INDIA AND SRI LANKA

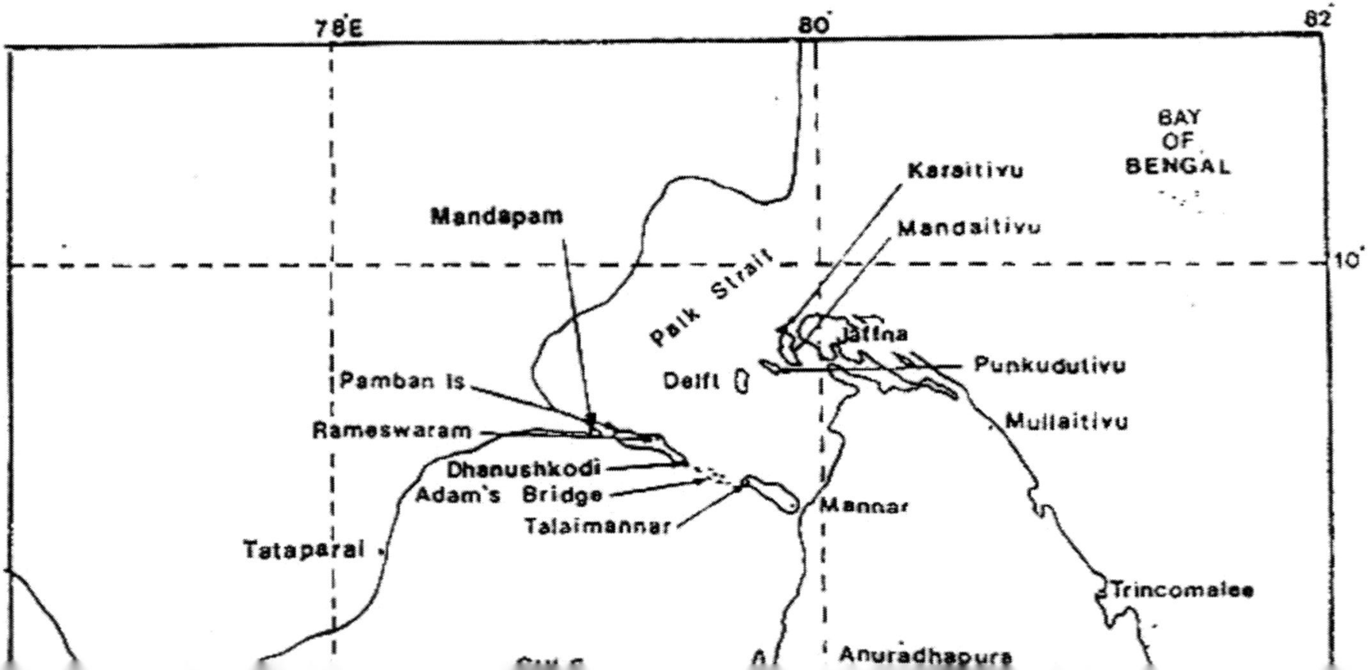

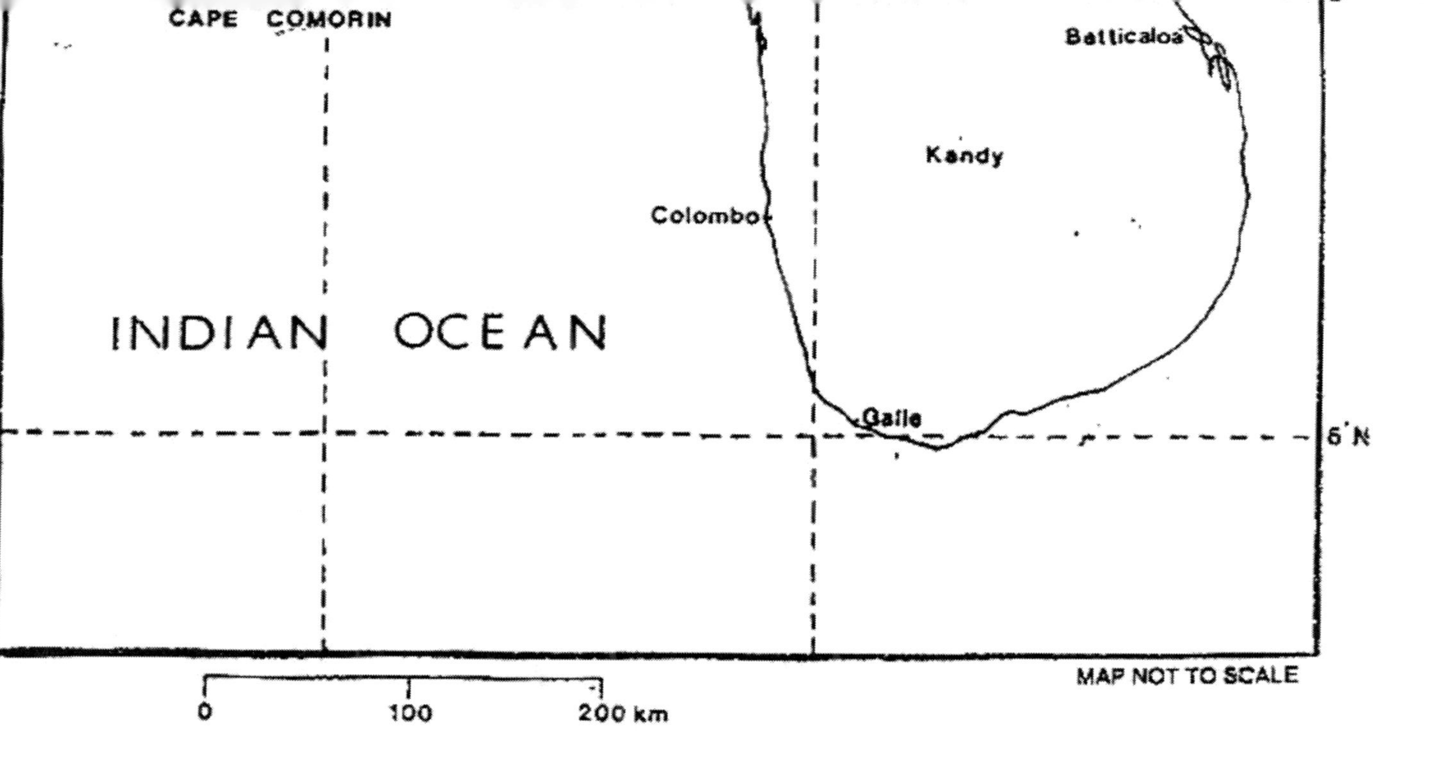
CAPE COMORIN
Batticaloa
Kandy
Colombo
Galle
INDIAN OCEAN
6°N
MAP NOT TO SCALE
0
100
200 km

SRI LANKA IN CRISIS
INDIA'S OPTIONS

BY THE SAME AUTHOR

Ayodhya: Ram Temple and Hindu Rennaissance

The Ideology of India's Modern Right

Hindus Under Siege: The Way Out

Economic Development and Reforms in India and China

Terrorism in India: A Strategy of Deterrence for India's National Security

Rama Setu: Symbol of National Unity

Corruption and Corporate Governance in India: Satyam, Spectrum and Sundaram

Hindutva and National Renaissance

India's China Strategic Perspective

Virat Hindu Identity: Concept and its Power

Building the Sri Rama Temple in Ayodhya

2G Spectrum Scam

SRI LANKA IN CRISIS
INDIA'S OPTIONS

Subramanian Swamy, Ph.D. (Harvard)

Member of Parliament, India
Former Union Cabinet Minister for
Commerce, Law & Justice, India

HAR-ANAND
PUBLICATIONS PVT LTD

Reprint, 2024

Published by Ashok Gosain and Ashish Gosain for
HAR-ANAND PUBLICATIONS PVT LTD
E-49/3, Okhla Industrial Area, Phase-II, New Delhi-110020
Tel: 41603490
E-mail: info@haranandbooks.com/haranand@rediffmail.com
Shop online at: www.haranandbooks.com

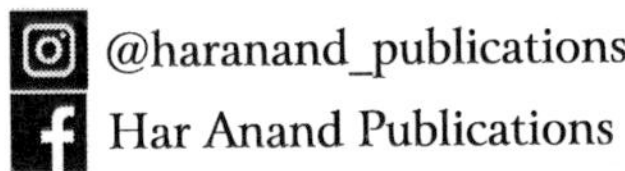

Printed in India

PREFACE

Why another book on the Sri Lanka crisis? Primarily for two reasons: first is that the crisis has deepened since the last book was written on the subject, and requires an urgent review of the genesis of the crisis shorn of all the mythology and propaganda; second, time is now at hand for Indian intervention for which there is widespread support from Sri Lankan civil society. So as not to repeat the errors of implementation of intervention committed in the past (1987-89), it is now essential to formulate an explicit policy framework for India's intervention. This book is about the genesis of the crisis, and proposes a clear cut alternative policy framework for Indian intervention in the Sri Lanka crisis.

Is the crisis rooted in religion, ethnicity, language or terrorism? We have to recognize that it is none of these. Certainly, there is no ethnic difference between Sinhalas and Tamils. The DNA structures are the same for the two communities. Nor is there any religious difference because Buddha is an avatar for the Hindus. The Sinhala and Tamil languages also belong to the same linguistic family as Sanskrit, and their respective scripts have evolved from Brahmi, and about 40 per cent of the vocabulary is common.

The origins of the current antagonism between the two communities, Sinhala and Tamil, is traceable however to the Sinhala perception of the Tamils' role during the colonial period and to the progress made by the Tamils enabled by the proximity enjoyed by the community as clerks and officers of the British-ruled administration. The Tamils put the opportunity to good use by accessing English education and the passport to employment that it entailed.

In brief, the Sinhala majority, as of now, does not want to share power with the minority Tamils by devolution in the Constitution. The day the Sinhalas develop sufficient self-confidence to do so, the crisis will abate. The Tamils do not want a separate Eelam except as a last option. They naturally do not want to suffer the terrible reverse discrimination anymore. They want the normal power sharing possible in civilized democratic society.

There is also a deeper subconscious apprehension in the Sinhala psyche about the Tamil demand for greater devolution: their own "minority complex." Though the Sinhala community constitutes over 75 per cent of the population of Sri Lanka, it views the Tamils not as a minority but as part of the looming Tamil political and demographic presence to the north of the island in Indian peninsular area of Tamil Nadu, which has a population of over 65 million, and seen as the natural support base for Sri Lankan Tamils. This makes the Sinhalas feel threatened by a possible dismemberment of their country—a division which could be initiated by India under pressure from its own Tamil citizens.

Thus, the problem in Sri Lanka, and why the island has been in crisis for over five decades, is not at all ethnic since there is no ethno-heterogeneity in the people. Nor is the problem religious because Hinduism and Buddhism, the two main belief systems of theology, are, at the very least, not mutually antagonistic. The latter is a reform of the former and respected as such. The Sri Lanka problem is instead a hangover of the British colonial mischief, and because the Sinhala community appears to bear a grudge against the Tamils for having got ahead by collaborating with the British colonialists.

It is, of course, ridiculous to bear this resentment even after sixty years of Sinhala dominated rule, but nevertheless it is there and needs to be addressed by India—if and when India intervenes for a solution.

There are today as many alternative solutions as there are parties to the strife. A feasible solution can, however, only emerge by first agreeing to who should be considered as the legitimate parties in the current crisis. Obviously, the easy answer is that the democratic elected government of Sri Lanka is one of the parties. The difficult question is who should represent the Tamils: whether it should be the LTTE, which seeks to be the sole representative of the Tamils, a claim surprisingly accepted by the fumbling clueless interlocutors from Norway, or whether there should be a composite negotiating partner of all Tamil parties as the present Government of India appears to favour, or that it should be a Tamil rainbow coalition but minus the LTTE, as this writer suggests.

It is my considered view that any alternative solution that includes the LTTE is doomed to failure and, more importantly, even if such a solution is found, it is against India's long-term national security interests. For India, I contend that a solution is feasible or viable only if the LTTE is excluded, and that LTTE has to be dealt with as a part of the problem, and not part of the solution.

Given this minimum precondition of excluding the LTTE from any solution, there is only one viable option for India. To make Sri Lanka to adopt an Indian-type quasi-federal Constitution for a united sovereign Sri Lanka. This is also the minimal demand of Tamils. We cannot go below this demand.

Time is at hand, therefore, for India to effectively contribute to the war against terrorism and in promotion of democracy by targeting the LTTE sincerely and effectively, which is also in the larger national interest of security and national integrity.

There is today a window of opportunity due to international consensus against the LTTE, and we must seize it now, provided the Sinhala majority overcomes its obdurate resistance to devolution, and takes the Tamils as equal partners in building the future of Sri Lanka as a democratic and peaceful nation. It is India's responsibility to persuade the Sri Lanka polity and civil society to accept this.

In writing this book, I have relied quite heavily on the research already done by other scholars. However, I have interpreted their data differently. Nevertheless I owe a debt to their painstaking research, and have acknowledged the same in the text wherever possible. My contribution, however, lies in framing the issues and suggesting an India-friendly solution that also meets the aspiration of the Sri Lankan people.

SUBRAMANIAN SWAMY

Contents

Chapter One

The Probem:
Terrorism—Is it Created by Differences in Religion or Language?

Sri Lanka is the name of the island situated off the southeastern coast of the Indian peninsula, separated by a 35 kilometre stretch of sea called the Palk Straits (see map on the end - paper). It lies between 6 and 10 degrees north of the Equator latitudes, and longitudes 79 and 81 degrees East. India's early Sanskrit scriptures had referred to the island as Sri Lanka, which the British colonialists who arrived in force in the eighteenth century, pronounced as Ceylon (Sri as "Cey" and Lanka as "lon"). For some time after becoming independent of the British in 1948, the island retained the anglicized name of Ceylon for some years.

In 1972, in the nation's new Republican Constitution, the name "Sri Lanka" was formally and officially re-adopted. The nation has predominantly two different language groups, comprising the Sinhala and the Tamil speaking peoples. The Sinhala people who constitute nearly three-fourths of the total population, are mostly of the Buddhist faith, while the Tamils are largely of the Hindu faith. Both groups claim Indian ancestry, the Sinhalas claiming to hail from the eastern part of India and the Tamils from the south eastern coast.

Today, the island is in a state of crisis; and, generally, this crisis is held to have arisen from "ethnic strife" and/or "religious animosity."

It is neither. International interlocutors or facilitators have been floundering in their peace efforts because they have wrongly understood the problem and the island's history.

The urgent need today is for India to correctly define its Sri Lanka policy and delineate it's options, precisely because India has a special responsibility due to her unique relationship with Sri Lanka, viz. as geographical neighbours, cultural siblings, and historical cohorts, and because of the national security implications of a festering crisis in the island.

The people of Bihar, Orissa, and West Bengal have umbilical links with the majority Sinhala community which constitutes 74 per cent of Sri Lanka's total population. The people of Tamil Nadu just across the Palk Strait have long-standing and continuing links with the minority Sri Lankan Tamils which links go many ages back. Hence India can play an effective role to stem the crisis in the island since the two nations are bonded together by history, culture, and geography.

The original basic sources of Sri Lankan history are the *Mahavamsa* and the *Chulavamsa,* which reveal that a prince either from Bengal, Orissa or Bihar had conquered the island and "pacified" the original tribal population: Prince Vijay Sinha reportedly had come with 700-odd followers to Sri Lanka around the third century B.C. to settle in the island and found a kingdom. The name Sinhala is said have evolved from the King's name "Sinha," which in Sanskrit signifies "lion." However, this version of Sri Lanka's history has not been corroborated by any other source.

The people of Sri Lanka were converted to Buddhism by Prince Mahendra (Mahinda in Pali), said to be the son of Emperor Asoka, who had gone to the island as a Buddhist missionary. By modern research in Indian history, that would place the date around 1600 B.C. Sri Lankans however still follow the British version of chronology, and place Buddha's *nirvana* at 483 B.C. Asoka's reign was 150 years later according to this chronology. Thus it is probable that Mahinda's ancestry traced to the Mauryan Kings of India is mythical.

Over the last two millennia, the majority of Sri Lanka's population became staunch followers of Hinayana Buddhism. The Tamil minority in the island are mostly of the Hindu faith, which religion in India had later assimilated Buddhism, as well as influenced what was left of it. Mahayana Buddhism, a synthesis of orthodox Buddhism and Hinduism became almost indistinguishable from Hindu theology.

There are today sections of Christians and Muslims also amongst the Sri Lankans, who should be recognized as separate entities even if these two communities are either Sinhala or Tamil speaking.

The Tamil presence in Sri Lanka, particularly in the northern region, dates back more than 2,000 years. At some periods, the northern areas of Sri Lanka were part of various South Indian empires; at others, they formed one or more independent Tamil kingdoms—especially the Kingdom of Jaffna. Just as Tamil Nadu and the other southern states of India converted to Buddhism, and then Jainism, only to return to mainstream Hinduism because of the efforts of Adi Sankara, similarly northern Sri Lanka also was once a Buddhist area, when Tamils had embraced that religion. The writings of Dr. Paul E. Pieris and Paulinus Tambimuttu document this fact.

Till the arrival of the Portuguese and Dutch in the sixteenth and seventeenth centuries, Sinhala kingdoms had coexisted with the Tamil ones of the north, and strife was limited to the usual kingdom rivalries. Antagonism between the Tamils, who were Hindus, and the Sinhalas who were Buddhists, was rare; it appears only in the legend of the fight between the Sinhala King Dutagamanu and the Tamil King Ellara.

The island was, however, fragmented dynastically and politically till the British arrived and defeated the Sinhalese king of Kandy in the late eighteenth century. As elsewhere, the British imperialists went about setting up a unified administration for exploitation of the natural resources of Sri Lanka. For this purpose, their experience of the British in India, enabled the Sri Lankan Tamils to quickly relate to their new masters. When they landed on the island, the British employers and traders already knew enough of the Tamil language to communicate with the local Tamils.

The origins of the current antagonism between the two communities, Sinhala and Tamil, is traceable to the Sinhala perception of the comprador role of the Tamils during the colonial period: the perception is that the consequent progress made by the Tamils was enabled by the proximity enjoyed by the community, as clerks and officers of the British-ruled administration. The Tamils put this opportunity to good use by accessing English education and the passport to employment that it entailed.

When Independence came in 1948, the Tamils dominated most of the professions and the government administration. The disadvantaged Sinhalas resented the progress made by the Tamils as the comprador class of the colonial period, but Independence provided to the majority Sinhala population the power of the state to rapidly close the gap by an autocratic policy of reverse discrimination. *This short-sighted policy is at the core of the problem today.*

The result of the British-Tamil collaboration was that the Tamils, despite being a minority had become disproportionately influential in the management of the Sri Lankan political and economic affairs right till the time of the country's independence in 1948. The Tamils became better educated; and they were also economically successful in the more remunerative non-agricultural sectors of Sri Lankan society. The antagonism was compounded by the Sinhalese feeling of being discriminated against by the British; and that this unfair treatment was done with the support of Tamils. This antagonism is at the root of the Sinhala resistance to constitutional devolution of power to Tamil populated areas: the Sinhala perception is that this is a measure that would freeze if not widen the gap between the Sinhalas and the Tamils.

A deeper subconscious apprehension in the Sinhala psyche about Sri Lanka Tamils' demand for greater devolution, is their "minority complex." Though the Sinhala community constitutes over 74 per cent of the population of Sri Lanka, it views the Tamils not as a minority but as part of the looming Tamil political and demographic presence to the north of the island i.e. in the Indian peninsular area of Tamil Nadu, a state with a Tamil population of more than 65 million, which is seen as the natural support base for Sri Lankan Tamils. This makes the Sinhalas feel threatened by a possible dismemberment of their country—a division which could be initiated by India under pressure from its own Tamil citizens.

The Sinhalas are thus in a Catch-22 fix—if they do not practice reverse discrimination then the Tamil-Sinhala economic gap will not be bridged, and Tamil minority domination in professions and administration would continue; and if they do practice it, then the Tamil community will continue to be alienated, and their plight might invite the intervention of India.

There is, however, no ethnicity involved in the Sri Lanka crisis. Tamils and Sinhalas in Sri Lanka are of the same ethnicity, and are of the same DNA structure as Indians. The problem today is best characterized as majority chauvinism fanned by antagonism of one community, the Sinhalas, and their fears about the future of the same majority community, of being swamped by India in support of the minority Sri Lankan Tamils.

Thus, the core cause of the Sri Lanka strife is not ethnicity, but a misplaced hegemony contrived on a distinction of language. It can therefore at most be labeled as a linguistic problem; but even here, not because the two languages are very different (*In fact, they are not so very different*) but only as a way to label the two communities at war with each other for reasons of recent history.

Because the Sinhala aversion to respond spontaneously to any just Tamil demand for devolution of power or autonomy, is rooted in the perceived role of the Tamils during the colonial period and the moral patronage that Sri Lankan Tamils could get from the huge Tamil population next door, therefore India needs to constantly address this apprehension without sacrificing the right to champion the human rights of the Tamil minority. What is to be cured is the minority complex of the Sinhala majority that forces it to deny basic human rights to the Tamils. For, in a democracy, no basic human rights of a minority can be allowed to be trampled upon by a brute majority.

Definition of a Minority

Of course, in a modern democracy, generally decisions on governance issues are determined by counting heads—as representing "the will of the people," the opinion of the majority of the people. The problem arises when the minority and the majority are distinct mutually antagonistic communities. Every such society then needs a federal Constitution with a "basic structure," i.e. a Bill of Rights which cannot be amended by any legislature on a majority vote.

In a democracy based on the rule of the majority, the protection of minorities is not a matter of compassion of the majority. The reason is that the concept of modern democracy itself lays down the legal basis for minority rights. Human rights in a democracy are held to be inalienable—part of the basic structure so that no human being could be deprived of those rights in a democracy by the will of the majority of the sovereign people.

This is the basic governance norm of democracy that was forgotten in Sri Lanka by the majority—the Sinhala language-based community, while dealing with the minority which is Tamil language-based.

Who are Minorities?

As noted jurist, Fali Nariman had observed, there is no universally accepted definition of the term "minority"! In fact, in some countries there is no equivalent for the word. The Government of Thailand in a communication to the U.N. Sub-Commission on Prevention of Discrimination and Protection of Minorities has stated that the concept of minorities is unknown in the country: "Although this word has a Thai translation from English for the purpose of communication with the outside world, it has no social or cultural connotation whatever." In most of the Latin American countries, the existence of ethnic or linguistic minorities is not recognized at all in the municipal laws. The Brazilian Government has gone on record asserting that there are no ethnic or linguistic minorities in Brazil, since immigrants are treated in the same manner as Brazilians. (Does the minority status then depend on the way a minority is treated?)

In a published United Nations study, the following definition of a minority has been suggested: "an ethnic, religious, or linguistic minority is a group numerically smaller than the rest of the population of the State to which it belongs and possessing cultural, physical, or historical characteristics, a religion or a language different from those of the rest of the population"! [E/CN Sub. 2/348 Rev. 1; UN (1979)].

By this definition, there are no minorities in Sri Lanka! Even the linguistic label suggested by this author above, is artificial, and has been inflicted on the island by British colonialists and their comprador historians. Sinhala and Tamil languages both have deep connection with Sanskrit and with Brahmi script. Nor can it be said that Hindu and Buddhist religions are antagonistic theologies. Buddha was a Hindu by birth, and had never repudiated the core concepts of Hinduism. He was a reformer and opposed to orthodoxy. Hindus accept him as an incarnation of Vishnu and revere him.

Moreover, a "minority" group in the sociological sense is not always a persecuted minority of the population; a majority of the people in a country may be in need of greater protection because of their status as a political minority or because of a policy of "institutional racism," e.g. the non-European majority people of South Africa during its period of Apartheid. The Hindus in Mughal India, and the indigenous population of Taiwan are other instances. On the other hand, the Parsis of India are a very small minority but have felt so comfortable with the Hindus that they have declined to accept any minority safeguards or affirmative measures.

The UN definition of minority also excludes migratory groups forced to leave their homes on account of unemployment or persecution—sometimes both. The immigrants and refugees cannot be ignored in any study on the protection of minorities.

In the pan-Asian context, I would submit that every distinctive disadvantaged group (whether religious, ethnic, linguistic, or socially and educationally backward) may be regarded as a "minority," and worthy of human rights safeguards.

In Sri Lanka, about three-fourths of the population is Sinhala and professes Buddhism; Tamils form twenty four per cent of the population, of which more than half are Sri Lankan Tamils whose forefathers have been in the island for hundreds of years possibly even earlier to the Sinhala migration from North India; the rest of them are "plantation" workers also known as "estate" Tamils or "Indian" Tamils since they were descendents of those brought over by the British as industrial labour in the last century. The latter group would also include those Muslims, mostly traders, whose mother tongue is Tamil. At the time of independence in the late nineteen forties, the northern "Ceylon" Tamil population held a disproportionately high percentage of employment in the civil services and were predominant in educational institutions for reasons stated above. The Sinhala antagonism has been towards the northern Tamils, but they also showed their wrath on the poor

"Indian" Tamils because of their Tamil language. The Sinhala after Independence disenfranchised these Tamils, and demanded that they be repatriated to India!

The first Constitution of Ceylon in 1948 although a unitary one, had contained a clause protecting the rights of the minorities, viz. Section 29 of the "Soulbury" Constitution (so called after its draftsman Lord Soulbury). But sometime after independence, the Sinhala majority got irrationally aggressive and adopted two policies that have been the source of much discontent amongst Tamils (and later cause of much violence): a "Sinhala only" language policy for administration and education, and "standardization" of marks: to qualify for entrance to universities, the lower marks of the Sinhala student were held equal to the higher marks of the Tamil student by a percentage mark-up.

At the time of independence, the Tamils had 32 per cent of the voting power in the Legislature. Upon the disenfranchisement of the "Estate" Tamils (who worked on the plantations) the percentage dropped to 20 per cent. At the General Elections, the Sinhala majority secured more than a two-thirds majority in Parliament. Then came the new Constitution of 1972, adopted by the predominantly Sinhalese Parliament in which Section 29 of the "Soulbury Constitution" was deleted. With the constitutional protection thus being denied, and the Tamils increasingly portrayed as "foreigners" whether north or south, the minority Tamils became restive, and one event cascaded into another, leading inevitably to violence by the end of the 1970s. In a study prepared for the Minority Rights Group, Walter Schwarz prophetically wrote in 1975:

> If Sri Lanka is not to experience communal violence or terrorism... there will have to be more readiness for compromise and modernization than has yet been shown—It would be a pity if Sri Lanka's leadership waited for bombs to explode and for the

prisons to fill up again before conceding that the Tamils need reassurance that they have a place in the future of the Island.

Lack of appreciation by the Sinhala majority, of the perils of such a conflict, led to the Tamil-Sinhala riots of July-August 1981 and then to the more shocking near genocidal events of July 1983 when Sinhala mobs massacred thousands of helpless and innocent Tamils. India's direct intervention followed this horrible genocide of Tamils. *The year, 1983 may be thus taken as a turning point and defining moment for the current Sri Lankan crisis.*

The problem thus is embedded in the island's history, and not in ethnicity, religion or even language. And the failure particularly on the part of the Sinhala majority, to compromise, to resile from falsely based positions, and to learn from history, is at the root of the Sri Lanka crisis today.

Sri Lanka's Early History

Until the beginning of the 16th century, much of present-day Sri Lanka was a pawn in the power struggles of the south Indian Tamil kingdoms of Pandya, Chola and Chera. During the four and a half centuries of European rule, (beginning with the Portuguese conquest of maritime areas in 1505, and culminating in the British conquest in 1796), the island had acquired its multi-religious and linguistic structure, the two well-demarcated linguistic cultures of Sinhala and Tamil, and the four religions: Hinduism, Buddhism, Christianity and Islam. While the island as a natural geographical unit imposed a certain unity on the people, their diverse cultures arising from colonial history forged separate collective identities and solidarities.

The outstanding fact of Sri Lanka's nationality structure prior to imperialist onslaught, is that from ancient times and continuously over the last two millennia, the two major linguistic groups—the Sinhala and the Tamil—have lived in and shared the country as co-settlers. This shared descent is traceable to the 2nd century B.C. or even earlier. The history of the people before that time has not been unravelled on a valid historical basis and is wrapped up in myths and legends invented by the Pali chronicles of the Sinhala people—the *Dipavamsa* and *Mahavamsa*—written in about the 4th and 6th centuries A.D., respectively. Both these chronicles are verse compositions in Pali, the Buddhist scriptural language, written by Buddhist monks, not in the historical tradition but as being the words of Mahanama, the author of *Mahavamsa,* "for the serene joy and emotion of the pious." They were written unabashedly from the Buddhist standpoint, lauding the victories of the Sinhala kings over the Tamil kings, treating the former as protectors of Buddhism and saviours of the Sinhalese, while deriding the latter as invaders, vandals, marauders and heathens.

In an effort to establish that the Sinhala are the original occupiers of the island, the chronicles misrepresent the Naga and Yaksha (or Raksa) Tamil people as non-humans, and validate their version by creating myths about the past. As Walter Schwarz, a perceptive writer on Sri Lanka, has observed: "The most important effect of the early history on the minority problem of today is not in the facts but in the myths that surround them, particularly on the Sinhalese side."

Sinhalese and Tamils—Origin, Myth and Truth

It is not established on reliable historical records when and how the Sinhala community emerged as a distinct linguistic group in the island. There exists no historical evidence for a Sinhala presence before the period when Buddhism emerged in India. The place of evidence has been taken by the King Vijay Sinha legend, that appears in the mythological *Dipavamsa* [literally "The Story of the Island"], written in the 4th century A.D. It purports to narrate the story of the island from the earliest human times.

The *Dipavamsa* introduces Vijay, as the first occupant and founder of the Sinhala, in these words: "This was the island of Lanka called Sinhala after the lion. Listen to this chronicle of the origin of the island which I narrate." According to the chronicle, on being banished for misconduct by his father Sinhabahu (the lion-armed), Vijay the grandson of a union between a lioness and the petty Indian king of Sinhapura came with 700 men in ships and landed on the west coast of Lanka, at a place called Tambapanni, in 543 B.C., on the day Buddha died, i.e. passed into *nibbana [nirvana in Sanskrit]*. (Incidentally, the correct date for Buddha's *Nirvana* is circa 1800 B.C.) Vijay's men were lured into a cave and captured by a demoness (Yaksha) queen named Kuveni. Vijay rescued his men, married Kuveni and had a son and daughter.

King Vijay later told Kuveni that before being crowned King of Lanka he should marry a human princess. He, therefore, banished Kuveni and the children into the jungles, and proposed marriage to the daughter of the Pandyan King. (Pandyans ruled the Madurai kingdom in south India). His men also obtained their wives from the Madurai region. Kuveni was later killed by demons. In the jungles, the children married incestuously and had many children, from whom, the chronicle states, the Veddas of Sri Lanka arose.

King Vijay is said to have held his coronation and made himself the king of Lanka and ruled for 38 years from Tambapanni, his capital. He and the Tamil princess had no children and hence, on his death, his brother's son Pandu Vasudeva came from Bengal and became the King of Lanka. This story has been retold with greater embellishment in the *Mahavamsa,* i.e. in *The Great Dynasty* (written in the 6th century A.D.), the source of the present-day early history of Sri Lanka.

However, there seems to be no historical evidence for the arrival of Prince Vijay and the related stories. There is no trace of a place named Sinhapura or of the petty king Sinhabahu in Bengali or

Oriya or Bihari history. But because of their inability to account historically for the emergence of the Sinhala, historians follow the lead of the Vijay legend.

On the basis of this legend, the present-day Sinhalas claim that they are the earliest settlers and are of "Aryan" origin. The foremost propagandist of the Sinhala-Buddhist "revival," Anagarika Dharmapala, wrote as long ago as in 1902 on the origin of the Sinhala as follows:

> Two thousand four hundred and forty-six years ago a colony of Aryans from the city of Sinhapura in Bengal ... sailed in a vessel in search of fresh pastures.... The descendants of the Aryan colonists were called Sinhala after their city Sinhapura, which was founded by Sinhabahu, the lion-armed king. The descendants of the lion-armed are the present Sinhalese.

But it is an undeniable fact that, in the ancient period of the island (*c* 1000-100 B.C.), there were two Naga kingdoms, one in the north called Naga Tivu in Tamil (and called Naga Dipa in the Indian Sanskrit works) and the other in the south-west, in Kelaniya. Even the Pali chronicles mention them in a different context, in connection with the purported visits of Buddha to the island. The *Mahabharata and Ramayana,* the two great epics written in Sanskrit, mention the Naga kingdoms and their conquest by Ravana, the Tamil Yaksha king of Lanka. So does the Greek astronomer and geographer Ptolemy, writing in the 2nd century A.D., who refers to Naga Dipa in the north, covering the territory from Chilaw in the west to below Trincomalee in the east.

Ptolemy describes the Tamil Yaksha people: "The ears of both men and women are very large, in which they wear earrings ornamented with precious stones."

Ptolemy refers to Naga kingdoms on the Coromandel coast; and towns with synonyms like Nagar Koil and Naga Patinam, appearing from the earliest times, confirm that Naga people of the same origin occupied the Tamil areas of south India and Sri Lanka. The latter may have migrated from south India in early times, when Sri Lanka was joined to mainland India through the shallow ridge of sandbanks called Adam's (or Rama's) Bridge in the Gulf of Mannar. Furthermore, the important find of a statuette of Lakshmi, the Hindu goddess of good fortune, in the Anaikoddai excavation (1982) confirms other evidence that the Naga people were Hindus and that Hinduism was the religion of the people of Sri Lanka before the introduction of its offshoot religion of Buddhism.

The conclusions that could validly be drawn from the new historical data clearly establish that the ancestors of the present-day Tamils were the original occupiers of the island, long before 543 B.C., which the Pali chronicles date as the earliest human habitation of Sri Lanka.

How, then, does one explain the emergence of the Sinhalese as an entity in the island? In the 3rd century B.C. (the date usually assigned is 247 B.C.), Buddhism was introduced into the island by missionaries led by *bhikkhu* (Buddhist monk) Mahinda. It is doubtful if he was the son of Asoka, the great Emperor of India (who modern research places at *c* 1500 B.C.). Mahinda, after being converted to Buddhism was determined to crusade for the religion abroad. Devanampriya Theesan, the Tamil Hindu king of Lanka at that time, accepted the missionaries and he himself converted to Buddhism. Since, the religion of the ruler became the religion of the people then and because Hinduism has never been antithetical to Buddhism, the new religion spread more as a reform of Hinduism than as an antithetical theology in the island.

Mahinda brought not only the religious message but also the Pali canon, i.e. the scriptures as preached by Buddha in Pali. The Buddha *dhamma* (the doctrine comprising the moral order), or at least the basic "five precepts," were taught to the people in Pali, and they are still recited by the Buddhists in Pali. The *Sangha* (the order of Buddhist monks), whose prerogative it was to know and preach the doctrine, learnt Pali in order to understand the *dhamma* as well as the *Vinaya* (rules of discipline for the *Sangha*). In this way, with Buddhism there come to Sri Lanka, came new language Pali; and it was learnt by the *bhikkhus* to preach the *dhamma* as well as for the writing of books, just as Latin was used by the Christian clergy in medieval Europe. In India, in the meantime, Sanskrit was re-throned by the continuous "Sanskritization" of Pali's vocabulary. Pali in India soon became indistinguishable from Sanskrit and was easily replaced by Sanskrit.

In the course of time, the Sinhala language as well as the alphabet and the script grew from the Pali language. With the spread of Buddhism and the growth of the Prakritic Sinhala language, there occurred a linguistic division of the people into those who remained Hindu and spoke Tamils and the emergent Buddhists speaking the Sinhala language. There is so evidence whatsoever of the Sinhala as a people, or Sinhala as a language, before Buddhism arrived in 247 B.C.

Nevertheless, even today, in their practice of Buddhism, the Sinhala Buddhist have not given up their Hindu past. They continue to worship the Hindu deities even though Buddhism opposes idol worship.

Even the caste system, prevails among the Sinhala Buddhists, although Buddhism is opposed to caste. One of the factors mentioned in the Sri Lanka media, as prejudicial to President Premadasa, was that the "upper caste" Sinhalas did not accept his "lower caste" leadership.

Taken together, the conclusion is clearly that Sinhala people in terms of their origin, are not "Aryan" as Sinhala intellectuals proudly claim but of Indian origin who adopted a language which developed from Pali. The Sri Lanka divide is not "ethnic," but can at most be labeled as linguistic. Even that difference is not much because Sinhala, Tamil, Pali and Sanskrit are all members of the same family of languages. They all use scripts that evolved out of the original Brahmi script.

This formulation thus rejects the mischievous British colonialist projection of Sri Lanka as a racially fractured society. There is therefore no truth that the present-day Sinhala has a distinctive racial Sinhala ethnicity different from Tamils. These two community differentiated only by language are inter-changeable ethnically. A Tamil person speaking Sinhala language and a Sinhala person speaking Tamil, have the same origins: one becomes a Sinhala, the other a Tamil because of his or her mother-tongue.

Between the 14th and the 18th centuries, large numbers of persons from Kerala, mostly from the Malabar area came and settled in the island. They were assimilated as Sinhala. So also did the "Colombo Chetties," whose ancestors came from the Chettiar community, in Tirunelveli district of Tamil Nadu (owing to a great famine there in the 17th century). The Sinhala cuisine even today reflects this connection.

In 1739, since Sri Narendrasinghe, the Sinhala king of the Kandyan kingdom, had no son to succeed him so the brother of his Tamil queen (from the Nayaka royal dynasty in Madurai) ascended the throne and took on the Sinhala name Sri Vijaya Rajasinghe. The succession of "Tamil" Kings continued until the Kandyan kingdom was ceded to the British in 1815. The kings of the Nayaka dynasty had merged thoroughly, taking Sinhala names and "converting" to Buddhism. So did their courtiers and retinue, who came over in substantial numbers.

Hence, in terms of identification and self-image, a Sinhala Sri Lankan person is one who bears a Sinhala name, and speaks the Sinhala language, while a Tamil Sri Lankan is one who speaks Tamil and bears a Tamil name whatever his origins may be.

The current "ethnic" problem of Sri Lanka is the outcome of the bogus history of the Island foisted by imperialist to further their divide and rule policy.

Even religious identification of Sri Lankan people as Buddhists and Hindus cannot be a basis of antagonism since Buddha is venerated by Hindus. For example, Indian law has a common civil code for the two religions. No Hindu would fight a Buddhist for religious reasons and vice versa.

Buddhism and Hinduism were also the only religions of the island until, following upon the Portuguese conquest of the littoral areas in 1505, Catholicism was introduced by the Portuguese, and despite all the persecution only a minority of the Sinhala Buddhists and Hindu Tamils converted to it. Later, under the British conquest and occupation (1796-1947), there were further conversions to Protestant Christianity particularly of the English-educated elite. Today, in Sri Lanka 67.4 per cent are Buddhists (all Sinhala), 17.6 per cent are Hindus (all Tamils), 7.1 per cent are Muslims, 6.4 per cent are Catholics and 1.4 per cent are Protestant Christians. 93.5 per cent of Sinhalas are Buddhists and 6.5 per cent are Catholics or Protestant Christians. Of the Tamils, 81 per cent are Hindus and the rest are Muslims, Catholic or Protestant Christians.

Unfortunately, the Sri Lanka people have allowed religious division to take place in such a way that being a Buddhist implies being a Sinhala, and being a Hindu implies being a Tamil. But despite this mischief from this contrasting configuration, there has been no known conflict between the two communities on religious grounds! On the other hand between the Buddhists and Muslims there have been conflicts, such as the 1915 riots. There were clashes between the Sinhala Buddhists and Sinhala Catholics in the early 1960s over Catholic dominance of the public and defence services, over education and over what the Buddhists objected to as the Catholic clergy "representing a foreign power" and engaging in "Catholic action," i.e. insidious priestly intervention in the recruitment and promotion of Catholics in government jobs.

The *Mahavamsa* links the "mythological origin" of the King Vijay, through a series of religious myths regarding the place of Buddhism in Lanka, as if these were ordained by Buddha himself. According to the chronicle, King Vijay Sinha landed in Sri Lanka on the day Buddha passed into *nibbana* (nirvana in Sanskrit). These two events are recorded as having occurred in 543 B.C. But modern research places the date that Buddha attained Nirvana as 1803 B.C., not 543 B.C. The chronicle states: "The prince named Vijay, the valiant, landed in Lanka, in the region called Tambapanni on the day the *Tathagatha* (another name for Buddha) lay down between two twin-like sala trees to pass into *nibbana.*"

In this way, the chronicle vests with a religious significance the arrival of King Vijay Sinha. The assertion in the chronicle that Buddha, just before his death, summoned Sakka, the king of gods and the divine protector of the *sasana* (the *dhamma* doctrine as taught by Buddha), and instructed him: "Vijaya, son of Sinhabahu, has come to Lanka together with 700 followers. In Lanka, O Lord of Gods, my religion be established and therefore carefully protect him with his followers and Lanka." By such imaginary injunctions of the Buddha, the chronicle vested Vijay and his supposed descendants—the Sinhala Buddhists—as "a chosen people" with the special mission of preserving the Buddhist religion in Sri Lanka, and not allowing others to corrupt or pollute their society.

The chroniclers of Mahavamsa thus falsified not only the early history of the island but even the Buddha's *nibbana.* They wrongly took 543 B.C. as the year of Buddha's *nibbana* and made the supposed arrival of King Vijay Sinha coincide with it. On the distortion of historical events by *Mahavamsa,* H. Parker in *Ancient Ceylon* observes:

> Tissa ascended the throne in 245 B.C. and is said to have reigned for 40 years; but this cannot be trusted, as the reign of kings who lived about the time have been extended to make the supposed arrival of the first Magadh [Bihar] settlers under Vijay, synchronise with the very doubtful date adopted by the Sinhalese

historians as the time when Buddha attained *Nirvana* or died, viz. 543 B.C.

Dr. Walpola Rahula, the scholar monk, wrote (1956) that "for more than two millennia the Sinhalese have been inspired that they were a nation brought into being for the definite purpose of carrying the torch lit by Buddha."

Tamil Identity

The Sri Lanka Tamils of today are of course the decendants of the original inhabitants of the island. The latter-day invasions by the armies of the south Indian Tamil Kings, the Pandyan, Chola and Chera kings, and by the Sinhalese kings, made additions.

At the advent of Buddhism in Sri Lanka (in circa 3rd century B.C.), the Tamil Kingdom was centred in Anuradhapura. Devanampriya Theesan, the Tamil king at that time, was followed by Senan and Kuddikan (177-155 B.C.) and by Ellalan (145-101 B.C.). With the defeat of Ellalan by the Sinhala Prince Dutugemunu, in 101 B.C., Anuradhapura became the seat of a Sinhala dynasty.

The fact that Tamil kings reigned in Anuradhapura before the rise of the Sinhala dynasties is borne out by *Mahavamsa* itself. In Chapter 24, it is stated that when Prince Dutugemunu informed his father, King Kavantissa, ruler of the southern principality of Ruhuna, that he was going to war against the Tamils, his father wisely replied: "Let Tamils rule that side of the Maha Ganga [now Mahaweli Ganga] and the districts this side of the Maha Ganga are more than enough for us to rule."

The history of the Tamil people in Sri Lanka after Ellalan's death is discontinuous and obscure thereafter for a millennium. The Pali chronicles describe only the struggles of the Sinhala kings, and their war with invading South Indian Kings. In 1214 A.D., an independent Tamil kingdom, with its capital in Jaffna, came into existence, and thereafter two parallel historical records came into existence—one Sinhala and another Tamil.

From that time, Sri Lanka was divided into two linguistic groups; the Tamils in the north and east, and the Sinhalese in the south and west. This today is the origin of the perceived separateness of the Sinhalas and Tamils, Buddhists and Hindu, north and south Sri Lanka.

The emergence of Jaffna as a centre of Tamil might and sovereignty is attested by foreign travellers who chronicled their experiences. According to Ibn Battuta, a North African Muslim traveller who visited Sri Lanka in 1344, the Tamil king Ariya Chakravarti, whose royal palace was in Jaffna, was a powerful ruler who owned sea-going vessels and a cultured man who could even converse in Persian.

The Portuguese, however, in 1505 conquered the maritime Sinhalese kingdom of Kotte, near Colombo. For over a century they attempted to subjugate the Tamil kingdom in Jaffna but in vain.

The Portuguese then administered the Tamil "Jaffna Patnam," as a separate area from their Sinhala maritime possessions. The Dutch, who defeated the Portuguese consolidated this administrative practice. Holland ceded her possessions in Sri Lanka to the British in 1802. But, in 1833 the British unified the low-country Sinhalese, the Kandyan and Tamil areas for their colonial rule, under a single unitary political authority—"The government of Ceylon."

Throughout the British colonial period, the Sinhala and the Tamil peoples were "pacified" and reconciled to their subordination to the British raj. The subordination extended to Sinhala and Tamil, just as Buddhism and Hinduism were subordinated to Christianity.

"Indian" Tamils

After the British imperialists colonized the island, they began to require captive indentured labour for their plantations. The so-called "Indian Tamils" of today are the descendants of the workers brought from the Tamil areas of south India by the British planters from the 1840s, as cheap labour that was bereft of rights to protest, for the large scale coffee and later tea plantations in the hill country areas. Beginning with about 3,000 in 1839, the arrivals increased to 77,000 in 1814.

By the time of the 1911 census, the separately enumerated Indian Tamils had grown to 530,983 and even outnumbered the 528,024 Ceylon Tamils in the area of plantations. These workers were paid a pittance of a wage and housed in barrack-like ghettos, in back-to-back 10-by-12-feet "line" rooms within the estates. Nearly all of them were poor and illiterate and often belonged to lower-caste groups, incapable of protest or uprising against the appalling working conditions.

Socially, these "Indian Tamils" suffered the worst of both worlds. The Sinhalas perceived them as a slaving Tamil community and the Sri Lanka Tamils regarded them with condescension and did not want to be identified with them because their enslaved and miserable plight lowered the respect for Tamils in the eyes of the people. Although their enterprise and toil cleared the forests, hills and valleys of central Sri Lanka for planting and harvesting of coffee, tea, rubber and cocoa, and their cheap labour in fact laid the basis for the island's prosperity because of exports revenue from these products, nevertheless and despite this contribution, the Indian Tamils in human terms were a pathetic lot, and as a class, little better off than bonded slaves.

Till the Sinhala brutality and genocidal attacks on Tamils in 1983, the Indian Tamils did not express their collective identity in terms of language, culture or even religion. Despite the discrimination they faced even in getting citizenship and voting rights. They identified themselves as a class, as plantation workers. From the 1930s they came to be organized into trade unions allied to the left-wing political parties which eschewed their Tamil or Hindu identity. Their position as the proletarian force and their unionization, resulting in class solidarity and militancy, did bring substantial improvements in their previously exploited working life. But the blanket targeting of all Tamils by the Sinhala chauvinists changed all that: "Jaffna Tamils" and "Indian Tamils" became united as Tamils in the struggle for human rights.

Despite differences which had existed or surfaced between the leaders of the various religious groups in the period preceeding Independence, there had emerged during the Sri Lanka freedom movement a basic consensus around a Constitution framed to allay the apprehensions of the Tamil minorities [Article 29 of the Constitution of Sri Lanka, 1948 enshrined that concern]. This provision in the Constitution prohibited enactment of laws which were discriminatory as between the various communities. For a moment it had seemed that the newly independent Sri Lanka was at peace with itself. But in 1972 this hope went up in smoke when the 1948 Constitution was replaced by a "Sinhala Only" Constitution in which Article 29 was deleted.

A country which gained independence without bloodshed or even much of a struggle and mainly as a consequence of India's successful struggle against colonialism, however finds itself today torn apart by conflict and rocked by armed violence, death and destruction for no other reason except on a bogus and contrived concept of ethnicity.

The problem arises because of the identification of Sinhala majority interest with the national interest. This has been perceived by the Tamil minority as an assertion of Sinhala hegemony. The conflict arises because the majority Sinhala population suffer from nightmares of their total annihilation and extinction by a Tamil majority from across the narrow strait.

Now nearly sixty years after Independence, the conflict confronting Sri Lanka is more acute today than at any time in the past. This unresolved conflict has resulted in the loss of more than

70,000 lives, and destruction of property on a vast scale. It has left the country's economy in a shambles, created refugees inside and outside the country, set in motion a process of militarization alien to normal civilian life, and emaciated democracy as it had hitherto been known in Sri Lanka.

Sinhala Perceptions and Fears

In spite of the common and composite culture of Sri Lanka, a deep-rooted faith has been instilled among the Sinhalas that the island is a Sinhala-Buddhist country and that Tamils are either alien "Dravidians" or not acceptable as equal partners of Buddhists. This faith is further reinforced by the long-held popularised belief that Lord Buddha chose the Sinhalas to preserve Buddhism, and in Sri Lanka. While Buddhism is practiced throughout the world and is particularly strong in Asian countries, Sinhala Buddhists have always felt that they have a special role in the preservation of true Buddhism. Such perceptions have resulted in expressions of intolerance towards the island's minorities and their role in Sri Lanka.

Another paranoid attitude is reflected the dictum: "Sinhalese have only Sri Lanka: they have no other place to go to." In other words, Tamils do have another country to migrate to. This fear is further exacerbated by the presence of more than 65 million Tamils in neighbouring South India. Although the Sinhalas constitute an overall majority in the country, the existence of such a large number of Tamils in close proximity has helped to create a minority complex and a feeling of collective fear and grievance. This sense of fear is heightened by the past support given to Tamil extremist groups in Southern India by certain regional parties.

Besides this paranoia, the Sinhalas have a grievance that the Tamils received preferential treatment during the colonial period which placed Tamils ahead of Sinhalas. It is a fact that the Tamils did enjoy such preferential treatment , since the British imperialists were familiar with Tamils in India. If the Sinhalas had the same opportunity they too would have seized it. The English introduced an education system in the 19th century to provide suitably trained persons to run the machinery of government. Since most of the schools were built in Colombo or Jaffna, this gave the Tamil community a disproportionate share of places and virtually denied all access to the rural Sinhala population. Not surprisingly, by the end of the British period of rule, the civil service and the professions became dominated by the Tamils.

The effect of colonialism in Sri Lanka was to create deep social and economic cleavages in whatever little religious and cultural differences had existed between Sinhala and Tamils. The post-colonial history of Sri Lanka based on unsafeguarded majority rule, has been one of Sinhala dominated governments who have been "hell bent" on divesting Tamils of their past social and economic gains. Despite sixty years of Sinhala absolute power. "Tamil privileges" however remains today the core perception within the Sinhala majority. They have not been able to close the gap.

As stated above, Tamils of Sri Lanka can be categorized into two groups, the "Sri Lanka Tamils" who live largely in the north and east parts of the island and "Indian" or Plantation Tamils who live mostly in the south. The Sri Lanka Tamils represent 12.6 per cent of the population.

Today, after disenfranchisement, the Plantation Tamils Constitute 5.6 per cent of the population, they are the descendants of the people brought from India as indentured labour by the British about 150 years ago. They live mainly in the Central Highlands where the tea plantations are located.

With the grant of universal franchise and the one person one-vote principle, the Tamils fear of institutionalised discrimination by the Sinhala majority community came to be true. The developments since 1948, when Sri Lanka became Independent, and free from colonialism, confirm these fears. In fact, the warning signs of the Sinhala paranoia translating itself into a brute majority to discriminate against the Tamils came early in the 1930s.

The State Council of Sri Lanka was elected in 1931 on a limited electorate, and seven committee were then constituted. The Chairperson of these Committees constituted the Cabinet. In 1936, the majority of the Sinhalese members of the State Council saw to it that each of the Committees had a Sinhala majority which ensured that all the Chairpersons were Sinhalas. From then on until the general election in 1948, the Cabinet was composed of Sinhalas only except for one Tamil appointed in 1942.

Then came the gross human rights denial of the Plantation Tamils who constituted nearly a million people at Independence. With one stroke, they were deprived of their citizenship and nationality in 1948; and in the following year they were deprived of their voting rights.

From 1911 to 1963, the plantation Tamils had averaged between 10 and 15 per cent of the population their numbers rising from 500,000 in the 1911 census to just over a million in 1963. In 1969-70, they accounted for 1,162,300 persons constituting 9.4 per cent of the total population. [*Report of the Socio Economic Survey of Ceylon*, 1969-70, [Department of Census and Statistics, Colombo]. By the 1981 census, they numbered 825,233 or 5.6 per cent of the total Sri Lankan population of 14.85 million. The reduction in their numbers thus is attributed to the repatriation of a considerable number since 1964. Even today, the plantation Tamils constitute one of the more significant minorities in the population of Sri Lanka.

Although, by their labour, the plantation Tamils have contributed enormously to the country's national income, they have been largely excluded from participation in the political life of the country.

The Donoughmore Constitutional Reform Commission had in 1927 estimated that 40 per cent to 50 per cent of the Indian

Tamils could be regarded as permanent residents of Sri Lanka. The Jackson Report on Immigration in 1938 had estimated that 70 per cent to 80 per cent of Indian Tamils were permanently settled. At Independence in 1948 thereafter, nearly all, numbering about 900,000, were permanently settled in Sri Lanka. The Indian Tamils had voted in the 1931 and 1935 elections for the colonial State Council. In 1947, in elections for the first parliament, eight Indian Tamil members of parliament, of whom six were from the Ceylon Indian Congress (CIC), the political wing of their trade union in the plantations, were elected, and Tamil representation rose to 24 of the 95 elected members.

The first independent government of Sri Lanka, within the first year of assuming office, deprived the plantation Tamils of their nationality and citizenship by the enactment of the Ceylon Citizenship Act of 1948, and in the following year deprived them of their franchise through the Ceylon (Parliamentary Elections) Amendment Act of 1949. The Plantation Tamils were thus rendered stateless and voteless. The Indian government, which had a vital interest in Plantation Tamils, showed scant concern, and watched passively. The so-called Indian Tamils were abandoned and orphaned. In fact, soon the Indian government agreed even to repatriation of these Tamils.

The Tamil representation which was about 25 per cent in the Parliament at Independence was thus reduced by almost 50 per cent as a result of the deprivation of voting rights to the Plantation Tamils. Hence, the majority minded Sinhala community with 75 per cent of the population but with a persecution complex acquired from the past, began the process that later ensured that Tamils become aggressively alienated from the Sinhalas.

The Prime Minister in the 1950s, S.W.R.D. Bandaranaike, father of President Chandrika Kumaratunge, inaugurated the "Sinhala-only" policy in the mid-1950s. He was assassinated by a Buddhist monk in 1959 for not doing enough. In 1960, his widow Sirimavo became Prime Minister, and she immediately moved constitutionally, using her party's brute majority, to decimate the "Indian" or "Plantation Tamils." A million Tamils thus became "stateless"—neither Sri Lankan (despite being for generations in the island) nor citizens of India.

An agreement entered into between the Indian and Sri Lankan governments (called the Sirimavo Bandaranaike-Shastri Agreement) in 1964, provided for the repatriation of 525,000 plantation Tamils to India and for approximately 300,000 to remain in Sri Lanka to be granted citizenship on a gradual basis. The division was arrived at arbitrarily and without the consent of the plantation Tamils or their representatives. The Agreement has been partially implemented, and an estimated 350,000 have been "deported" to India while approximately 150,000 have been granted citizenship.

In January 1986, the Sri Lankan Parliament passed an Act granting citizenship of Sri Lanka to 469,000 stateless persons of Indian origin. This was a consequence of a greater activism on part of the government of India led by Rajiv Gandhi as Prime Minister. The Indo-Sri Lanka Agreement and the subsequent developments in the island have now helped to normalize the situation of the Indian or Plantation Tamils, the credit for which justifiably belongs to Rajiv Gandhi as Prime Minister of India.

After disenfranchising Plantation Tamils, Sinhala political parties welshed on the pre-independence understanding, that the Sinhala and Tamil languages would together replace English as the new official languages of the country. In 1954, the Sri Lanka Freedom Party (SLFP) and the then ruling United National Party (UNP), abandoned this two language policy and adopted the policy of Sinhala as the only official language. In June 1956, the Official Language Act was enacted declaring Sinhala as the only official language.

Having placed the Tamils at a disadvantage in terms of language, the Sinhala majority then moved to deprive them of a fair opportunity in government employment. Since Tamils were not landowners or estate lords or in the export business, for Tamils, state and private sector employment were the only avenue for economic survival and social advancement. Hence a large number of Tamils held administrative and clerical jobs at the time of Independence in Sri Lanka.

Thus, for the Tamil community which had relied heavily on employment as a means of economic survival, being deprived of this avenue by governmental discrimination, frustration and alienation was inevitable.

For example, of the nearly 500,000 vacancies filled in the state and corporation sectors after 1977, the Tamil community "qualified" for less than 2 per cent. Indeed since the 1970s, there had been an invisible moratorium on Tamils being selected for the armed services, and even recruitment of Tamils for the police force had been drastically reduced. Today Tamils constitute less than 2 per cent in the armed services and less than 5 per cent in the police service despite being 24 per cent overall in population. According to the Department of Census and Statistics, between the years 1977 and 1981, of 9,965 persons recruited into the clerical service, 9,326 (or 93.6 per cent) were Sinhalese and 492 (or 4.9 per cent) were Tamils. The unemployment rate among young Tamil males who had passed the G.C.E A/L Examination was 41 per cent during the 1970s and early 1980s. The Sinhala unemployed rate was 29 per cent despite being less educated.

One of the principal causes of the rise in adherence to militancy among the educated Tamil youth has been the frustration on the question of admission to higher education. One of the major points of tension among many Tamil youths has been the implicit quota in an university admission policy that barred many competent Tamil youths from pursuing higher education because of the "marks standardisation" rule whereby Tamil students had to obtain 25 per cent more marks to be considered equal to the Sinhala student for admission to universities and medical schools.

In the 1950s, jingoistic competition between the United National Party (UNP) and the Sri Lanka Freedom Party (SELP), on the alleged Tamil domination of the island's educational institutions and bureaucracy, laid the foundation for reverse discrimination by the State against the Community.

Sri Lanka and the "Indian" Muslims

The identity of the Tamil speaking Muslims (also called "Moors") of Sri Lanka is another anomaly in Sri Lanka. Though a few Muslims had come in the tenth century, as traders to the island, the Muslims became a distinct community only from about the 12th Century.

In the 1911 census, Muslims born in Sri Lanka became classified as "Ceylon Muslims," and those who acknowledged that they came for trade, and would return to India, as "Indian Muslims." In the 1971 census, Sri Lankan Muslims numbered 824,291, or 6.5 per cent of the total Sri Lanka population, and Indian Muslims 29,416, or 0.2 per cent. Today there are only Sri Lankan Muslims, and they constitute 6.7 per cent of the Sri Lankan population.

Even in the post-independence period, the Muslims have displayed a conservative political profile, never confrontational, but always seeking to maximize advantages in the shifting political landscape. They have single mindedly sought to maintain their entrenched role in the wholesale and retail trade and financed both UNP and SLFP. As a consequence there have been Muslim ministers in the cabinets of all governments since 1948, and between 1965 and 1970 there were 12 Muslim MPs although as a community they were a majority in only six constituencies.

In 1889, a controversy arose as to their "ethnicity." Muslim Tamils had hitherto been considered Tamils and the Muslims had willingly identified with that. In the then Legislature Council, one P. Ramanathan, argued that the Muslims had originated in south India, and were Tamils who had embraced Islam.

The Muslims perhaps encouraged by the British colonialists, soon enough thereafter sought to make out that their ancestors came as traders, or were the Hashemites who left Arabia in the 7th Century on account of persecution. They began distancing themselves from Tamils, who were being increasingly identified with a "Dravidian race," a myth concocted by the British.

Tamil is the mother tongue of nearly all the Muslims, but it is a pity that they do not seek their collective identity in language or culture but only in their religion—Islam.

Evolution of the Conflict

Thus, the problem in Sri Lanka, and why the island has been in crisis for five decades is not at all ethnic, since there is no ethno-heterogeneity in the people. Nor is the problem religious because Hinduism and Buddhism, the two main belief systems of theology are at the very least not mutually antagonistic. The latter is a reform of the former and respected as such. The Sri Lanka problem is a hangover of the British colonial mischief, and which can be labeled for convenience as linguistic since the two groups in conflict are separate language speaking groups, Sinhala (75 per cent) and Tamil (24 per cent). The two languages are also sisters and of the same parentage for their vocabulary, grammar, and respective scripts of common origin.

Because of the wide and deep commonality of origin, the solution to the Sri Lanka crisis lies in the simple device of devolution: federalism, or quasi-federalism. The US is the model for the former, and India for the latter. However, any proposal for devolution runs into the fear psychosis of both Tamils and Sinhalas. The latter fears devolution as being the fore runner of either secession of the Tamil areas, or for annexation by India. The Tamils fear the devolution proposals are just time-buying tactics of the Sinhala community to keep the international community pacified, and therefore short of a separate nation, Eelam, there is no long-term security. These fears feed on each other.

The Bandaranaike-Chelvanayakam Pact (July 1957) was the first attempt of the two linguistic communities to solve the problem by devolution. The pact between the then Prime Minister, S.W.R.D. Bandaranaike, and the then leader of the Tamil Federal Party, S.J.V. Chelvanayakam, *inter alia,* provided for a wide measure of autonomy through Regional Councils to be set up in the Tamil areas of the north and east. The Councils were to have powers over a wide range of subjects including agriculture, cooperatives, land and land development, colonisation, education, health, fisheries, housing, social services, electricity, water supplies and roads. It also provided for Tamil to be recognised as a language of the national Tamil minority of Sri Lanka and as the language of administration in the northern and eastern provinces. It further recognised that "early consideration" should be given to the question of Sri Lanka citizenship for plantation Tamils. Had this Pact been implemented, the country would have been spared much subsequent strife and violence.

However, no sooner was it signed than an island-wide campaign was, mounted by the then opposition United National Party (UNP) and the Buddhist clergy denouncing the pact as a "betrayal of the Sinhalese/Buddhist people." On 9 April 1958, a large number of leading Buddhist monks stormed the Prime Minister's residence and demanded that the Pact be abrogated forthwith. A besieged Prime Minister capitulated, but the monks insisted on getting this promise in writing. The Prime Minister obliged and gave the written pledge to the monks [*Emergency 1958* by Tarzie Vittachi].

In 1965, effort was made by the then leader of the UNP, Dudley Senanayake, and S.J.V. Chelvanayakam both as coalition partners in a new government. The provisions of this agreement were similar to but not as detailed as the earlier 1957 Pact. In part fulfilment of the agreement, the government introduced regulations for the "reasonable use of the Tamil language." The SLFP, in Opposition, now led by Bandaranaike's wife Sirimavo, in alliance with the

Buddhist clergy, replicated the earlier UNP/Buddhist operation in 1958, and mounted a campaign characterising the regulations as a "sell-out to the Tamils." Although the regulations received parliamentary approval, these were never implemented since the government failed to honour the provision of the Agreement by enacting appropriate legislation, the Federal Party of Chelvanayakam resigned from the government and went into opposition. The seeds were planted for polarisation and confrontation.

The United Front Government under SLFP led by Sirimavo Bandaranaike gained an absolute majority in the 1970 general elections. In a binge of chauvinism and short-sightedness the government introduced as "standardization" for university admissions, the marks equalization scheme, whereby a Tamil student was required to get 25 per cent more marks. Thus a further block was created on the employment prospects of Tamils. Thereafter the promulgation of the 1972 Republican Constitution thus contributed to a further widening of the differences between Tamils and Sinhalese, since it removed the vestiges of the theoretical protection accorded to the minorities in the Constitution of 1948. Article 29 of the 1948 Constitution had provided as follows.

1. Subject to the provisions of this Order, Parliament shall have power to make laws for the peace, order and good government of the island.
2. No such law shall—
   (a) prohibit or restrict the free exercise of any religion; or
   (b) make persons of any community or religion liable to disabilities or restrictions to which persons of other communities or religions are not made liable; or
   (c) confer on persons of any community or religion any privilege or advantage which is not conferred on persons of other communities or religions; or

   (d) alter the constitution of any religious body except with the consent of the governing authority of that body.

3. any law made in contravention of subsection (2) of this section shall, to the extent of such contravention, be void.

Not only was this Article dropped without any similar provision being substituted, but also the 1972 Constitution, *inter alia*, granted constitutional status to the Sinhala language as the sole Official Language. It also allocated to Buddhism the status of a state religion by giving it a "foremost place" and enjoining the state to afford protection to Buddhism.

Although the Tamil Federal Party (TFP) had, since its formation in 1949, adopted the position that Sri Lanka was comprised of two distinct communities, Sinhala and Tamil and, advocated a federal system of government as the most suitable constitutional structure for a country with two peoples speaking two different equal languages, it had, nevertheless, remained unreservedly opposed to a division or separation of the country. In the 1970 General Elections, the Federal party had made a categorical appeal to the Tamil people "not to lend their support to any political movement that advocates a bifurcation of the country." And the Tamil people supported the appeal in a very large measure by voting for the TFP.

The situation radically changed following the betrayal that the 1972 Constitution represented, of the promise made to the Tamil electorate. Chelvanayakam resigned his Parliament seat to challenge the Sinhala leadership to prove that the 1972 Constitution was acceptable to Tamils, by holding a by-election in which he would contest. *The Sinhala dominated government never held the by-election.*

In May 1972, a renewed sense of radical unity among the Tamils dawned with the formation of the Tamil United Front (later the Tamil United Liberation Front), an umbrella organisation of the main Tamil political parties. The TUF organised protest demonstrations and campaigns in the Tamil areas against the new

Constitution. Tamil youth campaigned strongly against the new Constitution. "Standardization" for admissions to universities was the trigger since it produced predictable resentment among the Tamil youth. The government responded with strong with draconian counter measures. Hundreds of Tamil youth were arrested and sent to prison without being charged. Allegations of torture were widespread. There soon emerged sections of the Tamil youth who reacted violently. For the first time in Sri Lankan Tamil politics, the use of violence in pursuit of political purposes began to emerge as a viable option, a phenomenon giving a new and alarming twist to the heightening conflict.

In May 1976, the TUF adopted a resolution which stated for the first time explicitly that the Tamils constituted a nation and that they had a right to self-determination. It committed itself to the "restoration and reconstitution of the Free, Sovereign, Secular, Socialist State of Tamil Eelam based on the right of self-determination inherent to every nation" and declared that such a state "has become inevitable in order to safeguard the very existence of the Tamil nation in this country" (Vaddukoddai Convention, 14 May 1976).

The TULF resolution also called upon the "Tamil youth in particular to come forward to throw themselves fully in the sacred fight for freedom and flinch not till the goal of a sovereign socialist state of Tamil Eelam is reached." This, although the Secretary General of the TULF M. Sivasithamparam declared, "ours is a non-violent, civil disobedience movement. According to in a letter to the Prime Minister, that the tenets of Gandhiji's teachings, we shall suffer whatever stern action you [Sinhalas] propose to take. History has also shown such sacrifices triumph in the end."

In 1977, the United National Party (UNP) led by J. R. Jayawardene won an unprecedented electoral victory in the General Elections to Parliament held in July 1977 winning 141 of the 168 seats in Parliament, The TULF too won from the Tamil dominated areas of the northeast, and became the largest opposition party. Amrithalingam became the Leader of the Opposition in Parliament.

A reorganized UNP under the leadership of Jayawardene as President, had recognised before the elections that "the lack of a solution to their problems has made the Tamil speaking people support even a movement for the creation of a separate state." The UNP manifesto upon which it secured its massive victory, *inter alia* also stated:

> The United National Party accepts the position that there are numerous problems confronting the Tamil speaking people. The lack of a solution to their problems has made the Tamil speaking people support even a movement for the creation of a separate state. In the interest of a national integration and unity so necessary for the economic development of the whole country, the Party feels such problems should be solved without loss of time. The party, when it comes to power will take all possible steps to remedy their grievances in such fields as:
>
> 1. Education
> 2. Colonization
> 3. Use of Tamil Language
> 4. Employment in the Public and Semi-Public Corporations.
>
> We shall summon an All Party Conference as stated earlier and implement its decisions. The decisions of an All Party Conference, which will be summoned to consider the problems of non-Sinhala speaking people will be included in the Constitution.

It is generally accepted that, except where the TULF candidates contested, the UNP received the largest number of Tamil votes. The Ceylon Workers Congress representing the bulk of the plantation Tamils also supported the UNP, and its leader, S. Thondaman, became a Cabinet Minister in the Jayawardene-led Government. The TULF, although having a mandate on its separatist platform, was also amenable to a negotiated solution.

A unique opportunity had thus arrived in which a fair and permanent solution to the Tamil problem could have been achieved through the means of sincere negotiation as promised by the UNP. The Parliamentary vote had established that Tamils as a community had a grievance. A time-bomb Tamil resentment was, however, ticking away that needed Sinhala sagacity to defuse it by sharing power with Tamils.

The Jayawardene Government did not summon its "round table conference" as promised. It pushed through instead the 1978 Republican Constitution within a matter of weeks when the country was still under a State of Emergency. The TULF urged that provision be made in the proposed Constitution for a measure of autonomy for the Tamil regions of the north and east. When this was rejected, the TULF MPs took no further part in the making of the Constitution. Thus, as in the case of the 1972 Constitution, the 1978 Constitution was also promulgated without the participation of the elected representatives of the Tamil people.

The pre-eminent and dominant Constitutional position given to the Sinhala language and Buddhism was ensured by making provision for Sinhala to be the sole official language and to "be the language of administration throughout Sri Lanka." It also enjoined that the State "shall give Buddhism the foremost place and accordingly it shall be the duty of the State to protect and foster the Buddha Sasana [Administration]." It also declared Sri Lanka to be a "Unitary State," thereby apparently diminishing any chance for a solution of the conflict by devolution.

Militant groups including the newly formed LTTE began depicting TULF leaders as capitulationists, as people who could be taken for a ride by the Sinhala leadership. They argued that only an armed rebellion can get Tamils justice, and Eelam was the only final answer.

Rioting broke out frequently thereafter, and the Sinhalas responded aggressively. Riots took place in 1977, 1979 and 1981.

But the worst was July 1983, which was state-encouraged if not sponsored: Tamils were hunted down and massacred, especially in Jaffna and Colombo.

When asked about the rampage against the Tamils in 1983, President Jayawardene unabashedly told Ian Ward, a British journalist, in these words: "I am not worried about the opinion of the Jaffna people.... Now we can't think of them Not about their lives or of their opinion about us." (*Daily Telegraph,* London, 11 July, 1983.)

His Ministers spewed even more crass comments about Tamils. The Government imposed strict censorship on all news relating to the Tamil people and operations of the army. On 22 July, the army in Jaffna abducted three Tamil girls and took them to their camps, and news spread that they had been raped and one of the girls had committed suicide. The following day the Tamil militant youths retaliated by throwing bombs into an army truck, killing 13 soldiers. The army went on the rampage, shooting people at random. In Manipay, the army shot and killed nine people, including six school children. In all, over 30 persons were shot and killed in Jaffna that day.

News of the killing of soldiers reached Colombo, and from 24 July, the worst ever anti-Tamil rioting started. Tamils were killed and hundreds of Tamil homes and shops were looted and burnt. Despite the declaration of an all day and night curfew, looting and burning continued for several days in the city, quite often in the presence of security forces. The area worst affected was Wellawatte, where Tamils lived in large numbers. The Tamil people fled from their homes to various refugee camps, some of which came under attack by the Sinhala mobs.

As a further retaliation, the government announced its plan in 1984 to settle Sinhala people in the predominantly Tamil north and east to make demographic changes that reflected the nationwide population ratio of 75 per cent Sinhalese to 25 per cent other minorities.

The Minister of National Security, Lalith Athulathmudali, explained that this operation was linked to the overall "ethnic" problem. He said: "I believe this is the successful method of combating terrorism in a non-violent way.... This could mean that somewhere in the future there could be more Sinhalese in the north than the Tamils." (*Democracy in Peril—Sri Lanka: A Country in Crisis* by Patricia Hyndman, Report of the Lawasia Human Rights Standing Committee, p. 19.)

President Jayawardene's view on the matter was contained in a PTI report of 22 January 1985: "That his government would carry forward the programme of settling Sinhalese in the north and east in accordance with the principle of distributing state land on the basis of ethnic proportion."

The government also commenced training and arming the Sinhala settlers in these areas. Weapons were distributed among the settlers for "self-protection." Advanced training was to be given to new settlers. One news report stated: "All able bodied persons going to the north to settle down will be trained in the use of arms and on defence tactics. Each family would have a three and a half acre piece of land to cultivate. The government would construct houses for them." (The *SUN,* Colombo, 19 January 1985.)

The effect of arming the Sinhalas in Tamil areas was to transform what was hitherto a conflict between the Tamil guerrillas and the security forces into an armed conflict between the civilian people of the two communities. What was up to some time ago, action by the security forces against the groups which had chosen to take up arms against the state, now became generalised fighting between two armed separate groups.

The tragic consequences of this move were seen during the latter half of 1985 particularly in the eastern province, when armed Sinhala settlers joined with the security forces in "anti-guerrilla" operations. A new dimension to the Sri Lanka crisis thus was added by the "settlement policy."

The violent events of July 1983 and the resulting flight of nearly 80,000 Tamils to the neighbouring South Indian State of Tamil Nadu, left India no alternative but to take an active role in the island. In August 1983, I had moved a Resolution in the Lok Sabha seeking India's armed intervention in Sri Lanka to protect Tamil human rights. Although the Resolution was defeated by the Congress majority, Mrs Gandhi as Prime Minister took the floor to "promise action." Mrs Gandhi's special envoy later visited Sri Lanka a number of times to discuss with the Sri Lanka government, major political parties and the Buddhist clergy, a possible solution.

But Mrs Gandhi was also not above playing politics. She despised Jayawardene personally, and saw the Sri Lankan crisis more as she had seen the East Pakistan crisis of 1971, as a way to put Jayawardene in a spot, and to support her pro-Soviet comrade, Ms Sirimavo Bandaranaike, then in the wilderness, deprived of voting rights on a criminal charge.

One disastrous decision Mrs Gandhi took, was to permit the training of Sri Lankan Tamil militant organizations on Indian soil. One such organisation took the training, and then turned terrorist and later rabidly anti-Indian—the LTTE.

After several rounds of discussions between her emissary, the Sri Lankan government leaders and the TULF, a document which came to be known as "Annexure C" was drawn up and finally agreed to by President Jayawardene when he visited New Delhi for the Commonwealth Leaders' Conference in November 1983. The contents of Annexure C were to be the basis for negotiations at an All Party Conference (APC) to be convened by President Jayawardene.

Annexure C, *inter alia,* provided for the following:

(a) District Councils were to be the basic unit of devolution. However, District Councils within a province may combine into one or more Regional Councils if the districts so desired and approved at a Referendum;

(b) in the case of the northern and eastern provinces, the union of the District Councils within each province was to be accepted;

(c) each Regional Council was to have a Committee of Ministers drawn from among the elected members and headed by a Chief Minister;

(d) the Regional Councils were to have legislative and executive powers over specified areas including internal law and order, justice, social and economic development, cultural matters and land policy. They would also have power to levy taxes and mobilise resources through loans in addition to receiving block grants from central government;

(e) membership of the armed forces should reflect the "ethnic" (*sic*) ratio and the police force in the north and east should reflect the ethnic (*sic*) ratio in those provinces;

(f) Subject to a national policy on land settlement to be worked out later, all settlement schemes should be based on ethnic proportion so as not to alter the demographic balance; agreement to be reached upon settlement schemes for major projects.

(g) The Constitution and other laws dealing with the official language Sinhala and the national language Tamil, the National Anthem and the National Flag, to be accepted.

Nine political parties were originally invited to participate in the APC which commenced on 10 January 1984. Later participation was widened to include the Buddhist, Christian, Muslim and Hindu clergies together with other interest groups. A Conference of political parties summoned to arrive at a political solution to the ethnic conflict was soon transformed into a conference of groups representing a multitude of conflicting vested interest groups.

Annexure C, which was agreed to by the President as the basis for negotiation, was later abandoned after objection to it was raised by

Buddhist organizations. The APC lasted throughout 1984 with postponements and long delays between meetings. The absence of the second largest Sinhalese political party, the Sri Lanka Freedom Party (SLFP), which boycotted the APC due to the fact that its leader Mrs Bandaranaike remained deprived of her political rights under an Election law and due to certain criminal cases foisted on her by the Government, seriously undermined any chances of solution based on consensus. The APC become a non-starter, a dead letter.

In the absence of an agreement between the participants, President Jayawardene chose unilaterally to submit proposals in the form of two draft Bills, describing them as the considered views emerging from the earlier Conference. The proposals included provision for 3,000 village-level local authorities, a further two tiers of District and Provincial Councils and also for the setting up of a second chamber of parliament to be called the Council of State, with 75 members, 50 of whom were to be nominated by the 25 District Councils and the balance by the President.

But his hardline Cabinet Minister, Cyril Mathew, publicly opposed the proposals and exhorted the Buddhist clergy to do likewise. The SLFP also rejected the proposals, characterising them as a "legislative give away" to the Tamils with nothing in return. The TULF too at the other end of the political spectrum considered the proposals inadequate and stated that they "did not embody any scheme of autonomy which could be accepted by the Tamil people"; but it did not rule out any further negotiations on the proposals.

On 26 December 1984, almost two months after Mrs Gandhi's assassination, President Jayawardene flatly announced that his government had decided not to go ahead with the proposals. He offered no other proposal or promises for the future. He probably thought that Mrs Gandhi's 40 year old son as Prime Minister was no match for him. Another opportunity for a peaceful negotiated resolution of the conflict was thus lost. From then on, Sri Lanka has been on a roller-coaster of crises. What became clear is that

Sri Lanka needed a facilitation and an umpire who understood the problem, and had enough influence to enforce an agreement. All past attempts at direct bilateral negotiations between the Government and the Tamil elected representations had failed because of Sinhala intransigience.

Thus, unaided negotiation, without mediators, was rejected as an option by the Tamils. Hence, external intervention became essential. After the July 1983 quasi-genocidal attacks on Tamils, India felt compelled to intervene because of her restive 60 million Tamils. India made the first formal attempt to mediate a negotiated settlement, in August 1985 at Thimpu, Bhutan.

At Thimpu, the Sri Lankan Government delegation put forward a draft legislation for devolution of powers. These proposals were only marginally different from the one rejected by the APC of 1984, and the TULF. As a consequence, Thimpu talks marked the first explicit articulation of the Tamil extremist position. In the joint statements issued by the composite Tamil delegation, including the LTTE, as well as the TULF, were three cardinal principles:

* Reorganization of the Sri Lankan state;
* Recognition of the existence of a Tamil homeland comprising the Northern and Easter provinces of Sri Lanka;
* Recognition of the right of self-determination of the Tamils in Sri Lanka.

Since any solution based on above listed three Thimpu principles could have led to Eelam by the backdoor, the talks failed. Besides, there was no scope for adjustment of views; these were so far apart.

But on one issue, a unanimity was achieved amongst the Tamils in the talks. India must stand guarantor of any agreement worked out in the future, and enforce such an agreement on all the parties. The LTTE delegation had also concurred. The IPKF, following the 1987 Indo-Sri Lanka Agreement, was dispatched in keeping with that commitment made to the Tamils delegations in Thimpu by the Indian Government. Now for the LTTE to claim that Rajiv Gandhi had to be assassinated, because he had dispatched the IPKF, is completely bogus, and a gross betrayal of India. In 1986, a Draft Framework of Terms and Understanding was worked out by India. This was accepted by Colombo as the basis for future negotiations. An untransigient Colombo was frightened into agreeing because when Indian Air Force jets dropped food packets in Jaffna following a Sri Lankan army blockade, the whole world watched mute in deafening silence. Jayawardene got the message: if India will intervene, no one else will bother.

Following the Draft Accord, the "*proximity talks*" commenced. The two sides to the conflict were in contact with India as mediator but did not engage in direct face-to face talks. This set the stage for the signing of the Indo-Sri Lanka Accord in the summer of 1987. It brought the deployment of the Indian Peace Keeping Force (IPKF) in the north and east of Sri Lanka to keep peace between the armed Tamil groups and the Sri Lankan armed forces and oversee the implementation of the Indo-Lankan Accord. Under the Accord, the Sri Lankan Government made a commitment to reform the state by creating institutions of regional autonomy in exchange for the end of the secessionist insurgency.

Political resistance in the South slowly forced the Sri Lankan Government to resile from its position. President Junius Jayawardene (1906-1996), who had signed the accord, was not too committed to it. In 1989, following the mounting cost in fighting the Tigers and facing opposition from Jayawardene's successor, President Ranasinghe Premadasa (1924-1993) who had entered into a clandestine agreement with the LTTE for supplying arms and money to fight the IPKF India decided to call off its forces from Sri Lanka. The IPKF withdrew in March 1990. This marked the *failure of another serious attempt at negotiating peace.* Focused entirely on the issue of withdrawal of the IPKF and the dissolution of the Eelam Peoples Revolutionary Liberation Front (EPRLF)-led North Eastern Provincial Council (NEPC), the Premadasa-LTTE talks of 1989-90 achieved little else and quite expectedly produced no settlement. Sri Lanka's return to war in 1990, after the IPKF pull-out, resulted in a cycle of failed peace attempts and war with greater intensity.

In 1994-95, another attempt at peace was made. Mrs Bandaranaike's daughter, Chandrika Kumaratunga of the Sri Lanka Freedom Party (SLFP), won the elections on a peace platform. Kumaratunga immediately began negotiations with the LTTE. She put forward a set of proposals for devolution of powers to the regions, which was a bold attempt to redress the imbalance in the relationship between the different groups. Both the proposals and constitutional reform initiatives submitted by her to Parliament were opposed by the opposition United National Party (UNP). This peace initiative collapsed as well in April 1995, resulting in a new cycle of war.

It took seven years of war for the Sri Lankan state and the LTTE to sign another ceasefire agreement and begin "peace talks" again in 2002. This ceasefire introduced the Norwegian as intermediaries. The Norwegian facilitation mooted by Chandrika Kumaratunga and the People's Alliance government in 1998, paved the way for a negotiated Memorandum of Understanding (MoU) signed formally on 22 February 2002. The MoU formalized a bilateral cease-fire (Cease-Fire Agreement or CFA) between the Government of Sri Lanka (GoSL) and the LTTE and attempted essentially at fostering an atmosphere conducive to negotiations. "Track One" phase of negotiations pertained to "process issues" and was regarded as the prelude to the second phase! "Track Two" was to address "core issues" of substance in resolving the conflict. The GoSL formally deproscribed the LTTE, which was a pre-condition for participation in peace talks, and talks were held in six rounds between September 2002 and April 2003. The LTTE, however, unilaterally pulled out of the talks (while reaffirming its commitment to uphold the Cease-Fire Agreement), proving the LTTE used the lull in fighting to recoup its loses, and was not interested in a solution. However, in the third round (at Oslo in December 2002), the LTTE made a substantive departure from Thimpu principle when it expressed its willingness to explore a solution founded on the principle of "internal" self-determination, and based on a federal structure within a united Sri Lanka. It was not clear if it was genuine departure from its earlier stand or simply to cater to an international consensus that Sri Lanka needs a Federal constitution instead of the current unitary one.

Tabular Summary of Peace Talks from September 2002-March 2003

16-18 September 2002	Sattashp Naval Base, Thailand	Set up Joint Task Force for humanitarian reconstruction in the North and the East
31 October-November 2002	Bangkok Rose, Garden, Thailand	Formed sub-committees, focused on humanitarian, de-escalation and Political issues.
2-5 December 2002	Oslo, Norway	LTTE decided to explore "a political solution within a united Sri Lanka."
6-9 January 2003	Bangkok Rose Garden, Thailand	To ensure the implementation of urgent humanitarian priorities.
7-8 February 2003	Berlin, Germany	Issues in relation to human rights.
18-21 March 2003	Hakone, Japan	In view of the confrontation at sea between the Sri Lankan Navy and the Sea Tigers both parties acknowledged the need for parallel progress in negotiations on security, economic and political issues.

Source: Podder, Sukanya, "Challenges to Peace Negotiations: The Srilankan Experience," *Strategic Analysis* (July-September 2006), Vol. 30, No. 3, IDSA, New Delhi.

Sceptics had warned that the LTTE was a hardcore insurgent outfit and would use the cease-fire agreement to regroup, rearm and renew hostilities. In this context, the Sri Lankan Tamil journalist and political analyst, D.B.S. Jeyaraj, wrote in 2003:

> Perplexing as its seems, indicators suggest that the LTTE has not revised its fundamental objectives but only engaged in a tractical shift as a political ploy.... If so, the LTTE game plan is clear. The proclaimed intention of seeking a federal solution is only for international consumption. It seems the Tigers want the negotiating process to fail at some stage without any blame attaching to them. The peace process should not arrive at logical conclusion; instead, it should collapse without a satisfactory solution being structured. If and when that happens, the LTTE would opt out and exercise its "right of external self-determination" and pursue a "secessionist war" again. "Pinpointing the failure of Colombo to arrive at a federal solution, the Tigers would assert that the Sinhala people were incapable of redressing and accommodating Tamil grievances and aspirations within a united Sri Lanka."

The break in talks following the LTTE pullout in April 2003 witnessed major upheavals. The "Tigers" suffered a split in their ranks following their eastern commander Col. Karuna's decision in the middle of 2003, to break from "the Wanni," or northern leadership. This infighting proved to be an important destabilizer further undermining the LTTE's claim of being the sole representative of Tamil aspirations.

The Sri Lankan political system today, based on the unitary Constitution of 1978, combines features of presidential and parliamentary forms of governments and thus there is a possibility of the two top executive positions (the President and Prime Minister) being held by two different political parties or alliances;

unlike in India where the President is not directly elected, and does not represent any party.

Subsequently, when the SLFP-led coalition formed a compact with the hardline Janata Vimukti Perumana (JVP) on 20 January 2004 the conflict between the President (SLFP) and Prime Minister (UNP) deepened. On 7 February 2004, President Kumaratunga dissolved Parliament and elections were held in April 2004. The new coalition, the SLFP-led UPFA, won the April elections to Parliament, and Mahinda Rajapakse of SLFP became Prime Minister.

In November 2005, the Presidential elections were held, and it resulted in the election of Mahinda Rajapakse of the Sri Lankan Freedom Party (SLFP) to Presidency. Rajapakse's razor-thin margin of victory in the November 2005 elections, according to some analysts, was ironically in a sense facilitated by the LTTE because the "Tigers" boycotted the elections in the North and East, thus denying Opposition candidate Ranil Wickremensinghe the deciding Tamil votes. The underlying strategy on the part of the "Tigers," was to avoid and dodge peace initiatives if SLFP-JVP came to power. In his so-called "Heroes Day" speech on 27 November 2005, LTTE supremo Vellupilai Prabhakaran (whose birthday it is) clearly threatened renewed hostilities: unless President Rajapakse came up with a peace initiatives to LTTE's liking. Otherwise, the "Tigers" would revive the struggle for Eelam within a year's time. The futile and inane Norwegian mediation continued, and talks were held at Geneva on 22-23 February 2006 with government's primary emphasis on reviewing the Cease-Fire Agreement (CFA), and the LTTE seeking the disarming of the "para militants" or, in other words, disarming the hated Karuna-faction in the eastern district.

The government is unwilling to agree to disarm the LTTE's "renegade" eastern commander, Karuna who is the proponent of Tamil grievances in the East, and has recently opened offices in government-controlled Batticaloa acerbated the tense situation. His "shadow" war against the "Tigers" is allegedly supported by the government and enjoys India's tacit support and complicity. The LTTE has failed to eliminate the Karuna challenge, and hence its demand that the Government disarm "paramilitaries" as precondition for talks. Both parties may have officially announced their compliance to the CFA, but the situation on the ground suggests that the cease-fire-which lasted for four years, now lies in shambles today. As Prabhakaran promised in 2005, a year later, in his 2006 "Heroes Day" speech he declared cease-fire as "defunct," and that there was "no alternative to Eelam."

As a consequence, the LTTE, after agreeing to a united Sri Lanka in 2002, had reverted to its strategy of achieving a Tamil Eelam through armed struggle. That is more or less the position today.

The Sinhala-Tamil divide for long was justified on this outrageously fraudulent basis of "racial differences" between "Sinhala Aryans" and "Tamil Dravidians." Now that the basis for that difference has been demolished by science, the supposed ethnic conceptualization of the crisis has dissolved. The Sri Lanka crisis is not ethnic in nature, since Sinhalas and Tamils are of the same ethnicity.

Nor is the divide due to religion since there is no fundamental theological difference between Hinduism and Buddhism. The supposed basis of antagonism between Sinhalas because they are Buddhist, and Tamils because they are Hindus, has evaporated as well. Buddhism had emerged from Hinduism as a reform theology. Hindus accept Buddhism completely, and regard Buddha as an *avatar.*

Even linguistically, the Sinhala and Tamil languages are sister languages in syntax, grammar and evocatives, and they share a huge proportion of the vocabulary common to Sanskrit. The scripts of both languages have evolved from Brahmi. Hence, the Sri Lanka crisis is linguistic only as a label, but not substantively.

The Sri Lanka crisis instead is due to the Sinhala inability to rise above their petty jealously about the Tamils' relative progress that they achieved by the accident of history of being co-opted by the British imperialists during their occupation of the island. Compounding this jealousy is the Sinhala "minority" complex arising from the presence of a large Tamil presence in the Indian mainland just 32 kilometers across the Palk Straits. Both these factors constitute a neurosis for the Sinhala people. Hence they refuse to grab the solution which is self-evident: a devolved Constitution on federal principles of the US or the Indian variety. Therein lies the crisis.

Chapter Two

The Alternative Solutions: Which is Feasible?

In Chapter One, we have formulated the problem underlying the current crisis in Sri Lanka *as ethnic or religious, as is normally portrayed, but it is one that can be labeled as linguistic.* The only relevant difference between the Sinhala majority and the Tamil minority in the island is the language they speak. Even the languages they speak, Sinhala and Tamil, have common Sanskrit vocabulary, and scripts descended from Brahmi.

The problem's root is the Sinhala majority's "minority complex," this arising from Tamils being their neighbours on the Indian mainland and being six times larger. There is also a past resentment amongst the Sinhala majority about the advancements and benefits in professions and education that the Tamils had reaped in collaborating with the British colonialists. It is of course ridiculous to bear such resentment after sixty years of Sinhala dominated rule, but nevertheless it is there and needs to be addressed.

There are today as many alternative solutions suggested for the problem as there are parties to the strife that are claiming attention for recognition. What is a feasible solution can only emerge by first deciding who should be considered as the legitimate parties in the current crisis.

Obviously, no solution is feasible without the democratically elected government of Sri Lanka as a party. The Sri Lanka Government is, however, essentially the elected representatives of the Sinhala majority. *The difficult question is who should represent the Tamils:* Whether it should be the LTTE which seeks to be the sole representative of the Tamils (a claim *defacto* accepted by the fumbling clueless interlocutors from Norway and Japan), or weather there should be a composite negotiating partner consisting of all Tamil parties (as the present Government of India appears to favour), or whether it should be a Tamil rainbow coalition *but minus the LTTE*, as this author proposes.

It is argued here by this author that any alternative solution that includes the LTTE is doomed to failure and more importantly, is also against India's integrity, sovereignty and long-term national security interests. *I contend that for India, a solution is feasible only if the LTTE is excluded, and that LTTE has to be dealt with as a part of the problem, and not a part of the solution.*

The question then is: why the LTTE is part of the problem in Sri Lanka, and cannot be part of a just solution? For this, we must understand the LTTE, and the implications of Rajiv Gandhi's assassination for India.

The Rise of the LTTE

The Liberation Tigers of Tamil Eelam's stated goals are: (1) A single Party [LTTE's] Marxist Eelam nation, and (2) that its leader, Prabhakaran, be regarded as the sole spokesperson (In fact, LTTE websites proclaim him as "Ulaga Tamizha Thalaivar," i.e. leader of all Tamils the world over!), and the LTTE as the sole organization of all Tamils of Sri Lanka. That is, an LTTE-led, single party, Marxist state with Prabhakaran as the dictator is their aim. It does not believe in a multi-party democracy. Can India permit such a formation in our proximate neighbourhood? Is this what the Tamils of Sri Lanka want? No freedom-loving people would trade one dictatorship or hegemony for another. And no nation interested in safeguarding its national security will allow the LTTE anywhere near it. The rise of the LTTE is a saga soaked in innocent human blood. It has risen to this position by brazenly killing anyone, Tamil or Sinhala, who differed with them on their goals.

In the late 1960s, Nadaraja Thangavelu (alias Thangadurai), Selvaraja Yogachandran (alias Kuttimani), and others formed the Tamil Eelam Liberation Organization (TELO), a militant alternative to the Federal Party. Later in 1983 this was taken over by Sabarathnam; and with Indian training, it blossomed into a powerful fighting machine, to the envy of Prabhakaran.

In 1973, the Tamil Students League leader Satyaseelam had been arrested by police, which led to a wave of repression, culminating in a number of young people being sent to prison. But Kuttimani fled to Tamil Nadu in India. But soon he was extradited to Colombo by the DMK Government! Kuttimani was sent to jail in Jaffna. Such was the apathy with regard to Sri Lanka Tamils even amongst Tamil chauvinist parties in India. Advocates of Tamil "pride" in India such as Karunanidhi were indifferent to the happenings in Sri Lanka then.

From 1978 to 1982, a London-based communist, a Tamil by name Eliathambi Ratnasabhapathy, had arranged for batches of 16 LTTE recruits to be trained in Lebanon by the Palestine Liberation Organization (PLO). It was George Habash's PLFP that trained them. This training was stopped when Israel invaded Lebanon in 1982, and arrested all sixteen recruits.

Interestingly, some of the current Congress leaders also has had long-standing relations with George Habash. This fact was revealed to me when I met PLO leader Yassir Arafat in Tunis, Tunisia, in October 1990, on behalf of Rajiv Gandhi.

A crucial impetus to Tamil militancy in Sri Lanka was provided by the anti-Tamil riots of July 1983, and the massacre of a number of militant leaders (including Kuttimani and Thangadurai in Sri Lanka's Welikade prison, following the ambush of a Sri Lankan Army patrol on the Jaffna-Palali road). This led to nearly one lakh refugees fleeing to India across the Palk Strait. Most of the refugees went to Tamil Nadu just thirty-two kilometres across.

According to one estimate, at the time of the Welikade prison massacre (1983), the LTTE had just forty fighters; but the riots led to a spurt in recruitment. The LTTE had first come to the notice of Indian authorities following the shootout between Velupillai Prabhakaran, the LTTE leader, and Uma Maheshwaran, the leader of the PLOTE, in Madras in 1982. The two leaders and their associates (who had been in India since mid-1981) had been out on bail until Prabhakaran jumped bail and escaped to Jaffna the following year. An arrest warrant on this is still pending: it has been kept pending on RAW intervention ever since Prabhakaran had re-surfaced in Pondicherry at the end of 1982.

It was around this time that New Delhi took an interest in the activities of the militants, especially after the massacre of Tamils in July 1983. Some of the Tamil groups, like LTTE, EROS, EPRLF, and PLOTE, had already received training from the PLO and the PFLP in the mid-1970s. The training that the Indians imparted was more extensive and involved all the major groups including the LTTE and the TELO. The Indian intelligence organization trained them in camps in Tamil Nadu, Karnataka, New Delhi, and in Chakrata in Uttar Pradesh. Simultaneously, camps sprang up in Tamil Nadu, where mass training of cadres began. The PLOTE and TELO trained the largest number, perhaps some five thousand persons in about fifteen well-run camps. The LTTE had camps in Salem and Madurai. Tamil Nadu Chief Minister and AIADMK supremo MGR established links with these groups to ensure that he was not personally outflanked on the emotive "Tamil" issue by his rival Karunanidhi. He proceeded to support first the PLOTE and then the LTTE with personal and government funds. This, in turn, encouraged a "competitive" Tamil jingoism between the two political rivals, which created the subsequent "India's Sri Lanka disaster" that the hasty withdrawal of IPKF in 1989 entailed.

Ironically instead of evolving to become the sole organization of the Tamils, the LTTE has become the undoing of the Tamil people, and even of the cause of Eelam itself that it espouses as its goal. The LTTE has in fact become a terrible albatross around the neck of the Tamil society of Sri Lanka.

Because of its terrorist activities, the LTTE today is also losing ground internationally, although it is still well placed in some countries such as Thailand, Italy, and South Africa. But its international base of operation now depends much on its involvement in the "narcotics running-for-guns" trade. Between 1994 and 2000, the LTTE had a frequent presence in Taliban-ruled Afghanistan and procured weapons from the Al Qaeda while providing training for suicide bombings. Representatives of the Saudi millionaire-terrorist Osama Bin Laden reportedly met LTTE persons in South Africa in November 1999. The journey from President Premadasa in 1989-90 to Osama in 1999-2000 has been a journey of utter opportunism by the LTTE. This terrorist organization's clandestine connection with the Al Qaeda has also been alleged in the British House of Lords by a peer. Since 1994, it is known to terrorist experts that LTTE maintains contact with the ISI of Pakistan (see appended news item).

Their military equipment ranges from locally manufactured heavy mortars and rocket-propelled grenades to heavy machine guns and shoulder-held SAMs obtained from worldwide clandestine arms markets. The weapons procurement logistic network headquartered in Phuket, Thailand, operates over the high seas through the use of eleven small freighters, from which the material is ferried in small fiberglass craft to the LTTE bases on the Jaffna coast. The operation is financed largely by narcotics running and trade.

Hence, not only is the LTTE a murderous ruthless organization, and anti-India, but it partners inside and outside Sri Lanka are all those who hate India and support terrorist activities inside India. It engages in narcotics trade, and is thus cash-rich. Some political parties in India rely on LTTE financing to fight elections. Hence, the LTTE can betray India at any time of its choosing.

The worst betrayal of India so far was when the LTTE teamed up with the Sinhala fanatic and President of Sri Lanka, Ranasinghe Premadasa, to ambush, kill and dishearten the IPKF soldiers who had come to Sri Lanka in 1987 to protect peace-loving Tamils against Sinhala fanaticism.

Premadasa became the President of Sri Lanka in December 1988 after J.R. Jayawardene (who signed the 1987 accord with Rajiv Gandhi) chose not to contest. Premadasa's stated aim was to restore peace in Sri Lanka by befriending the LTTE and JVP (a Sinhala extremist group). In April 1989, the LTTE agreed to talk to Premadasa and flew down a delegation from London to Colombo. The JVP, however, refused to make peace.

On 1 June 1989, Premadasa publicly asked the IPKF to quit Sri Lanka. Rajiv Gandhi refused, leading to a much-publicised war of words between the two. It was in this scenario that Premadasa decided, on LTTE's request, to supply it with arms and ammunition. Vivid details have been given in the affidavit of Lt. Jayath Vaithiyage of the Sri Lankan Rapid Deployment Force filed before the Commission of Inquiry investigating Premadasa's assassination.

The first supply of weapons was made in July 1989 at the Welioya army base in the country's north-east, adjoining Mullaitivu and Trincomalee districts. According to an army officer J.M. Bohoran (mentioned in the Premadasa Assassination Commission Report), one of the first consignments of weapons came in four trucks to the base. A handful of LTTE leaders, including the group's Paris-based international spokesman Lawrence Thilagar, also arrived there by Sri Lankan air force helicopters. With the help of a small unit of soldiers, the arms were moved to a place called Kent Farm.

The consignment included 500 T-56 automatic rifles from the Central Armoury at the army headquarters. Another consignment (two trucks) followed. They had 1,00,000 rounds of ammunition for self-loading rifles and 2,00,000 rounds for T-56 rifles. More than 100 LTTE cadres took delivery of the ammunition about 15 kilometres from the Welioya camp.

According to H.S.J. Udaya Kumara, chief inspector of the Special Task Force (STF), four LTTE guerillas stayed at the STF camp at Katukurunda (near Welioya) for more than six months (when the LTTE was battling the IPKF)! They were provided with "special accommodation." According to him, 400 T-81 rifles were also given to the LTTE. Lt. Vaithiyage told the Commission that the booty (which came in trucks covered with canopies and without number plates) also contained grenades and electric detonators and explosive (TNT and RDX) plastic. Later accounts showed that the "Tigers" were also given handcuffs and building material.

According to his Secretary Wijedasa, Premadasa "was insisting on arming the LTTE. All efforts of persuading the President to revise his decision failed. Officers thereafter complied. They also thought that by this means the IPKF would be forced to leave the country." The Commission says of Premadasa: "We thus see a man with faulty judgment taking momentous decisions affecting the country without heeding the advice of his selected lieutenants and without a proper understanding of the issues involved. He was surrounded by lackeys who did not dare to displease him" Defence Secretary Attygala stated in a poignant comment: "[We knew] the implications, if we didn't comply with Premadasa's orders." When one army officer complained to Defence Minister Ranjan Wijeratne about the dangerous implications, the latter argued that "the weapons will be used against the outside forces, the IPKF."

Lionel Karunasena of STF claimed that in early 1990 his men cleared electronic equipment imported into Sri Lanka for the LTTE. "The [Sri Lankan] armed forces," says the Commission, "turned a blind eye to this episode of arming the LTTE. The LTTE had hundreds of thousands of weapons but more were given by the government as they (LTTE) said they did not have enough." All this for fighting the IPKF, which was already on its way out. (The Indian army quit Sri Lanka in March 1990.) These weapons were later used by the LTTE against the Sri Lankan Army.

The Murderous Activities of the LTTE

The LTTE today is a banned terrorist organization in India, US, Canada, and UK and other countries. Led by V. Prabhakaran, the organization started on 5 May 1976 as a forty-man outfit. The supremo, Prabhakaran, was born on 26 November 1954, the youngest of four children, to a District Land Officer, Tiruvenkatam Velupillal and Vallipuriam Parvathi. After some school education in Batticaloa, he moved to Velvettitural, his native town. He surfaced on the media radar on 27 May 1975, when he is said to have shot dead the Jaffna Tamil Mayor, Duraiappa. Prabhakaran, however, owned up to the murder only on 25 April 1978 (when LTTE as an organization owned up to all 11 past murders!).

A bizarre feature of the LTTE tactic has been the use of suicide or *kamikazi* commandos, both men and women, some in their early teens, for individual assassination as well as for mass attacks. They kill those whom Prabhakaran does not fancy, Tamil and non-Tamil. In 1988 a Tamil lawyer, S. Nadarja, who had ably defended the LTTE in the 1975 Jaffna Mayor's assassination case, fell foul of Prabhakaran only because he had participated in the IPKF-organized Indian Independence Day celebrations! He was killed in cold blood.

What has also discredited the LTTE internationally is its terrible record of cold-blooded murders of individuals, mostly unarmed, who had sought peaceful resolution of the Sri Lankan strife, or fell foul of the LTTE for some other reason such as being pro-India. The murder of Tamil United Liberation Front (TULF) vice-President Neelan Tiruchelvam, who was sympathetic to them, *but not under their control,* earned the LTTE's ire only for that reason.

LTTE chief V. Prabhakaran (who is reputed to be the sole arbiter of who is to be assassinated) orders a person to be put on the hit list if (*a*) he/she is against the LTTE, (*b*) is pro-India, and (*c*) if he is a rival. All three categories are designated as "traitors" for the LTTE cadre. It does not matter for him if such a targeted person is for or against the creation of Eelam.

If indeed such is the murderous intent and anti-India motivation of the LTTE, why should India work for a solution of the Sri Lanka crisis if the LTTE is to be empowered or legitimized? Let us look at the LTTE's record of murders to see the pathological and obsessive desire to murder.

Beginning with the first entry in LTTE's "diary of murders"—that of Jaffna Mayor Alfred Duraiappa of the Sri Lanka Freedom Party on 27 July 1975—the murder spree is ghastly, and continues even today.

On 7 May 1986, the LTTE hunted down and shot dead Sri Sabarathnam, the charismatic leader of the Tamil Eelam Liberation Organization (TELO), as the organization's proximity to India posed a threat to the LTTE's passion for hegemony. Sri Sabarathnam was killed in a betel plantation in the Jaffna Peninsula. The "Tigers" then executed several hundred TELO militants and decimated the once powerful organization. TELO was till then the leading organization fighting for Eelam.

The LTTE later murdered pacifist leaders of the TULF: one after another, those who had pressed for a negotiated settlement as an alternative to the long-drawn-out war. On 13 July 1989, TULF Secretary-General A. Amirthalingam and Politbureau member V. Yogeswaran MP, were shot dead at the latter's home in Colombo by the LTTE militants, Visu and Aloysius. It was a typical LTTE operation. The two militants had earned the trust of Yogeswaran by meeting him frequently as part of the parleys to sort out the differences between the two groups, and they led him up the garden path. On that fateful day, when Visu, Aloysius and another LTTE militant Vignan came visiting, Yogeswaran, in a show of trust, told the security men not to frisk them. Vignan stayed at the gate, while the other two went in. A little later, Amirthalingam and TULF President, Sivasithamparam, joined Yogeswaran. Yogeswaran's wife, Sarojini, served them tea. Visu and Aloysius then opened fire killing Amirthalingam and Yogeswaran at the tea table. The reason for the killing? LTTE had taken umbrage at Amirthalingam's speech in the Sri Lankan Parliament in June 1989, pleading for the continued presence of the Indian Peace Keeping Force (IPKF) on the Island.

LTTE employed this lulling ploy later with Rajiv Gandhi too. In March 1991, the LTTE operative Kasi Anandan, through a well-known editor Ms Malini Parthasarathy's introduction, had met Rajiv Gandhi at his residence at 10 Janpath (see diary page of Rajiv Gandhi's engagement appended here). Later at the persuasion of a former Foreign Secretary, Rajiv Gandhi met LTTE's London-based chartered accountant Arjun Sithampalam. Both meetings were planned to make Rajiv Gandhi lower his guard, and collaterally to make him yield to persuasion, which was to come later from his dubious associates, to go to Sriperumbudur to address that fateful meeting on 21 May 1991.

While Rajiv Gandhi did not reveal his mind to LTTE's emissary, he did so to others. What was really on Rajiv Gandhi's mind was revealed, it is most probable, to a third person, one Rajarathinam of ENDLF, or to the TELO delegation which had met him even earlier on 30 January. One of the two outfits obviously had a LTTE mole, and thus Prabhakaran came to know what Rajiv Gandhi had in his mind about the LTTE if he came to power again. "Be patient till I come to power," Rajiv Gandhi had reportedly told Rajarathinam when the latter had complained about the LTTE. Prabhakaran understood what that meant.

The SIT chargesheet filed in the trial court of Rajiv Gandhi's murder described these meetings correctly as "smokescreens," as an alibi for a contingency. To quote the chargesheet: "As expected, holding of elections in May 1991 was officially declared in March 1991.... In March 1991, about 10 days apart, two emissaries of LTTE had separate secret meetings with Rajiv Gandhi in New

RAJIV GANDHI'S ENGAGEMENT DIARY
MAINTAINED BY VINCENT GEORGE

31 Days **MARCH 1991** 3rd month

5 Tuesday

0900 Chief Whips LS/RS, RDS, Salhi, HSS
GNA, PC, HKLB, PSS, RKD, MLF

0945 Parlty Mtg —

1100 MPs
↓
1400.

1600 CPP Executive Committee. —

1700 SS Rathee + Others of Delhi

1715 Kasi Anandan of LTTE
c/o Malini Parthasarathy

1730 Chinese delegation

1900 Veer Sanghvi Sunday

1915 General Secretaries AICC

2000 Anita Baweja

2000 W/o Bilchand daughter —

2115 D.B.

2200
↓ Subramanian Swamy + TNS

Delhi to fathom his mind, to ascertain whether there was any change in his attitude towards LTTE and also to create a smokescreen for their evil designs."

Just after the assassination, *Frontline* (8-21 June 1991) magazine interviewed the LTTE high-ranking leader based in London, known as "Kittu." According to the magazine: Kittu said Kasi Anandan did meet Rajiv Gandhi on behalf of the LTTE. "I gave him permission. I am a Central Committee member of the LTTE. He asked me whether he should meet Rajiv Gandhi, even to make arrangements to meet him. Rajiv Gandhi knew that Kasi Anandan is our political leader. Only after he knew it did he agree to see Kasi Anandan. The meeting lasted 45 minutes...." V. Prabhakaran's permission was also taken for Kasi Anandan to meet Rajiv Gandhi, Kittu said.

Kittu also revealed that Arjun Sithampalam, a charted accountant based in London, whom he described as an "international banker," met Rajiv Gandhi within two weeks after Kasi Anandan. But Sithampalam claimed to have met Rajiv Gandhi not on behalf of the LTTE, but "on behalf of the Tamils," a thin fig-leaf indeed.

Kasi Anandan, a member of the LTTE Central Committee, who surprisingly continues to live in Chennai, was summoned and deposed, at length, before the Jain Commission on 10 October 1996. Why the Jain Commission would summon a member of a banned terrorist organization to depose, is beyond anybody's comprehension. But the Jain Commission was being manipulated by certain persons with connections in high places, to see if the LTTE could be exonerated from the accusation of Rajiv Gandhi's assassination, and the dastardly deed of his murder be pinned on someone else.

According to Anandan, he had approached Ms Malini Parthasarathy, editor and part-owner of *The Hindu,* to get an appointment with Rajiv Gandhi, and this was fixed by Vincent George his P.A., for 1715 hours on 5 March 1991. I had met Rajiv Gandhi on the same day with T.N. Seshan and R.K. Dhawan for four hours from 2200 hours till 0200 hours, but Rajiv Gandhi did not tell us a word about the meeting. This is explicable only if non-political sources were behind the meetings. Ms Parthasarathy, although an educated person, was taken for a ride by Kasi Anandan. She obliged him and got him to meet Rajiv Gandhi, completely oblivious of the LTTE's planned perfidy.

Hence, as late as 25 May 1991, four days after the assassination, *The Hindu* was of the opinion that the LTTE, in view of the Rajiv Gandhi-Anandan meeting, had no incentive to kill Rajiv Gandhi. The newspaper corrected itself in ample measure soon enough, and fearlessly exposed the LTTE thereafter.

In his deposition, Kasi Anandan stated in his pigeon English as follows:

> ... I said to Ms Malini Parthasarathy that I will have to take permission from the LTTE Supremo.... She said that I should take the permission. She also said that she will also meet Rajiv Gandhi and get his approval for my meeting him. I passed the message to Prabhakaran through Kittu who was in London. I got Prabhakaran's approval from Kittu. I again met Malini Parthasarathy. She sought time from Rajiv Gandhi at his residence on 5 March 1991 in the evening. I came along with Sachidanandan to Delhi. It was a meeting, one to one. None else was present. It was a 45 minutes meeting. Nothing was recorded by Rajiv Gandhi. I told him that war had already taken place; there was a gap prevailing between LTTE and the Government of India and it should be bridged. There were negotiations with Sri Lankan governments, on earlier occasions, but nothing came out and we have been deceived. And I told him that we would not rely either on Sri Lankan leadership or Sri Lankan Constitution anymore. And it is India that should stand with us and solve the problem. He accepted the fact that we were deceived by the Sinhala Government. He also told me

> that he regretted very much for the past. He also promised that they would help us in our struggle. He did not tell that he will support Eelam.... Till that day I knew that he was opposing to Eelam. I went to Rajiv Gandhi with the purpose that he may support for a separate Eelam. *He did not agree to support for* [*sic*] *separate Eelam.*

Dr Arjun Sithampalam is a British national. He was informally examined in London by S.K. Datta, then Additional Director, CBI about his meeting with Rajiv Gandhi (Tour Note SIT File No. 153: Foreign Enquiries Reports of S.K. Datta, I.P.S., ADCBI).

According to the tour report, Dr Sithampalam stated that he had met Rajiv Gandhi on 15 March 1991. The meeting was fixed for 1145 to 1200 hours. Rajiv Gandhi was expecting him and shook hands on his arrival. They then sat and talked for 20 minutes and no notes or memos were taken or exchanged on either side.

Dr Arjun Sithampalam stated that the meeting with Rajiv Gandhi was on account of the fact that he might come to power. "*LTTE had friends in V.P. Singh's Cabinet" and the idea now was to "make bridges with RG in case he came to power."* For this he delivered a bland message of friendship from Kittu.

Dr Sithampalam had telephoned Kittu before the meeting. After the Rajiv Gandhi meeting on 15 March 1991, he returned to London. He reported back to Kittu on 18 March 1991 at Tavistock Place, London. This clearly establishes that Dr Sithampalam too was LTTE's stalking horse, and indicates similarities in the *modus operandi* of the two emissaries of LTTE. In both the instances, the permission was given by Kittu on behalf of the LTTE but sanctioned by Prabhakaran. The objective of the two meetings appears to be the same: *to make Rajiv Gandhi lower his guard against the LTTE, and to encourage him to come to Tamil Nadu for election campaigns.* The third and fourth meetings, either unwittingly or wittingly, served as a way to discern the inner thoughts of Rajiv Gandhi about the LTTE. Killing opponents and "betrayers" had become an obsession with Prabhakaran. But to execute his orders for assassination, to motivate his *kamikazes* to kill themselves for the cause, he needed an excuse. For Prabhakaran, being pro-India as Sabarathnam and Amirthalingam were was good enough for him to order assassination. Any subjective feeling of betrayal he hardboured (as in the case of Mahathiya) was sufficient excuse for him to murder a close associate. A person's being opposed to LTTE and positioned to ascend to power, even if (as in Rajiv Gandhi's case) this was only a conjecture, was sufficient for him to motivate suicide bombers.

Earlier, the LTTE had killed George, leader of the Eelam People's Revolutionary Liberation Front (EPRLF), and R.R. Vasudeva, a top People's Liberation Organization of Tamil Eelam (PLOTE) leader. The killings took place in Sri Lanka. But soon the LTTE had developed logistics and the gumption to carry out such murderous operations in Tamil Nadu as well. On 19 June 1990, the "Tigers" stormed into an apartment at Zacharia Colony in Kodambakkam, Chennai, when the central committee meeting of the rival EPRLF was underway, and sprayed bullets killing fourteen top EPRLF leaders, including its secretary-general K. Padmanabha, P. Kirubakaran, and Yogasankari MP. While escaping in a car after the attack, they killed two local people on the way. The killers were facilitated by the then DMK Government in Tamil Nadu to flee to the Vedaranyam coast of Tamil Nadu, and to the Jaffna peninsula from there with assistance from Shanmugham, a local Congress leader. This itself should have alerted any patriotic Indian in authority. But not Prime Minister V.P. Singh. He was soft on LTTE for his narrow political interests. Hence, the nation had to wait for the coming of a new government (in November 1990 headed by Chandrashekhar) for corrective action, to cleanse Tamil Nadu of LTTE's overt set-up in the state. I was Cabinet Minister for Law, and given the task to uproot the LTTE from Tamil Nadu, and within two months, I had accomplished the task.

The LTTE anger at EPRLF was only that the latter had backed the Indo-Sri Lanka Agreement (which pact was an object of hate for the LTTE since the Agreement failed to accord the status of "sole spokesman" for the Tamils to the LTTE). Moreover, the EPRLF ignored the LTTE's call to boycott the Northeastern Provincial Council elections in 1988. It participated in the elections and formed the Council with the Eelam National Democratic Liberation Front (ENDLF) headed by Paranthan Raj, an alias Gnanasekaran. This naturally upset the LTTE and it was biding it's time. When the EPRLF leaders came to Tamil Nadu after the IPKF pulled out of the island in March 1990, the LTTE struck.

Ranjan Wijeratne, Minister of State for Defence, was killed on 2 March 1991, when the planter-turned-politician was travelling in his bullet-proof *Mercedes Benz* car, in the heart of Colombo. The LTTE detonated about 100 kg of explosives planted in a parked car, killing the Minister, as his car passed by it. In this case, Prabhakaran seems to have been motivated by the betrayal by the Minister first in using the LTTE to fight IPKF, and then turning on them after IPKF withdrawal.

On 8 August 1992, ten top Sri Lankan Army officers including the Northern Commander Maj. Gen. Denzil Kobbekaduwa, and Maj. Gen. Wijeya Wimalaratne, Jaffna Area Commander, were killed when the jeep in which they were travelling at Araly Point (in the Kayts Island off the Jaffna peninsula) was blown up. LTTE supremo V. Prabhakaran owned the killing and furthermore was "pleased" that his militants had discovered a disused mine and had triggered it. He was happy to claim credit for it. But it all looked "too pat" as an American phrase goes. As M. R. Narayan Swamy in "Sri Lanka's Arming of LTTE against IPKF" [*Economic and Political Weekly*, 3.10.98] notes: "Kobbekaduwa was popular amongst Sinhalese people, and was to become Chief of Staff in Colombo in January 1983." A Commission of Inquiry headed by a Supreme Court Judge, instituted later in 1994 by the then newly elected President Chandrika Kumaratunga, however, concluded that the assassination was executed on *President Premadasa's orders,* and by the Sri Lanka Army. What is significant about the Commission's Reports is the set of documents it revealed on the LTTE-Premadasa collusion during the period when IPKF was in northern Sri Lanka.

The Commission's report states:

> From January 1990, Kobbekaduwa, Athulathmudali and Gamini Dissanayake were investigating the secret delivery of weapons, arms and ammunition, electric equipment, batteries, detonators, explosives, etc. Kobbekaduwa and the others wanted to place all of this before some international tribunal and had been in contact with foreign diplomats.... Exposure of all of the above would certainly mean political disaster for President Premadasa.

The Commission opined after examining various evidences that the killing was an inside job. It said there was no pressure mine, and the explosives which blew up the Land Rover, were hidden in the vehicle; that the track which the Land Rover used was not a disused one (as made out earlier) but was in constant use and— so a buried mine would have been easily detected. Furthermore, a soldier who took photographs of the explosion and its aftermath had his film roll removed from the camera and the pictures were never developed or made available to Investigators; no post-mortem was done on any of the dead officers; a mysterious doctor gave an equally mysterious injection to Kobbekaduwa while he lay almost dead at the airport tarmac; there was delay in removing the general to hospital; there was tampering of evidence—the crater for example was enlarged to prove it was a buried mine which caused the blast; and some evidence was not made available to earlier investigations.

The Commission concluded: "After careful consideration of all the evidence, real, direct, circumstantial ... oral, documentary and opinion evidence, of motive, opportunity and preparation ... this commission is able to come to one conclusion only and that is Premadasa himself targeted Kobbekaduwa for assassination .... The evidence proves beyond doubt that Premadasa was directly responsible for the assassination. Without political support at the highest level, the [defence] ministry and the army would not have got involved in murdering a national figure like Kobbekaduwa." Obviously, Prabhakaran wanted the LTTE to get free credit and psychic satisfaction in claiming responsibility for this assassination, in sharp contrast to denying, till it became impossible, any role in Rajiv Gandhi's assassination. The reasons are obvious. Killing Rajiv Gandhi had earned him the wrath of the Indian people, while killing a Sinhala figure enhanced his reputation with the Sri Lankan Tamils.

On 1 May 1993, the LTTE turned on their former ally President Ranasinghe Premadasa, and killed him at a May Day parade. In Central Colombo. Premadasa, sporting a green cap with "victory" written on it, was directing the United National Party's (UNP) procession. A youth with explosives strapped on to his body cycled towards the President and when securitymen stopped the bicycle, he detonated the device killing the President and 24 others. In 1989-90, incidentally, Premadasa was LTTE's open ally against IPKF. Interestingly, the killer had worked as a domestic servant in Premadasa's house for a number of years before. After the IPKF pullout, LTTE felt that Premadasa had betrayed them; so he was listed for assassination.

Gamini Dissanayake, the UNP's presidential candidate, had addressed an election meeting in a Colombo suburb, which concluded a little after midnight on 24 October 1994. Dissanayake checked the time on his watch and wished the gathering "good morning." An LTTE woman militant, who was sitting in the second row of the audience, stepped forward and exploded herself, killing Dissanayake and sixty others in the process. Dissanayake's only fault was that he was considered pro-India and had visited India prior to the campaign.

On 5 July 1997, Arunachalam Thangadurai, TULF's Trincomalee district MP, was about to get into a vehicle in Trincomalee town when three LTTE men lobbed a grenade and opened fire. The mild-mannered parliamentarian was killed instantaneously. In June 1990, a motorcycle-borne LTTE gunman killed Sam Thambimuttu, TULF MP from Batticaloa, and his wife Kala, outside the Canadian High Commission in Colombo. Both political leaders were not anti-LTTE, but discouraged violent methods in TULF ranks, and were sympathetic to India.

Jaffna Mayor Sarojini Yogeswaran, the widow of V. Yogeswaran (who was killed earlier in Amrithalingam's house), was felled by an LTTE hit man's bullets at her home in the Sri Lankan Army controlled Nallur in Jaffna town on 17 May 1998.

The killing spree has continued till today. Sri Lanka's Foreign Minister and a Tamil, Kadirgamar, was killed in 2005 at his residence because he had foolishly boasted that he was instrumental in getting the EU to pass a resolution against the LTTE. He had, of course, nothing to do with the EU's decision to ban the LTTE. Moreover, Kadirgamar was a Tamil in a Sinhala dominated government. This was not to the liking of the LTTE which seeks a polarized Sri Lanka, between the Sinhala and Tamils, with the LTTE as the "sole spokesman" of the latter.

This tragic chronicle of murders shows the deepening culture of violence in Sri Lanka. It is also partly an outcome of the brutalization of the Tamil psyche caused by the irrational hegemonism practised by Sinhala leaders that made "Gandhian" leaders Chelvanayakam and Amrithalingam look *effete* and ineffectual. But it is also in large measure due to the murderous mentality of the LTTE top leader V. Prabhakaran.

Moreover, as past history shows, Sinhala intellectuals have played into Prabhakaran's hands, by polarising the Sinhala-Tamil divide. Prabhakaran has flourished in this atmosphere of brutalization, and hence feels insecure and threatened if any attempt is made to harmonize and humanize the prevailing situation by bringing Tamils and Sinhalas together into a common identity.

In February 2000, former Prime Minister I.K. Gujral and a person who had hastened the withdrawal of the IPKF when he was Foreign Minister in the pro-LTTE V.P. Singh Government, got a sinister mouthful from the LTTE for daring to attend in Colombo a commemoration ceremony for Tiruchelvam. At the function, Gujral had praised President Chandrika too. The LTTE mouthpiece from Paris, *Eelamurasu,* called Gujral a "joker" and compared him to the assassinated Tiruchelvam as a "politician who enjoyed power through the back-door" and castigated both, ominously, for being "traitors to the Tamil cause." A grim warning indeed even if vulgarly worded. Obviously, the LTTE had thought of Gujral as "their man" till then (because of his role in IPKF pull out) and felt let down when he went to commemorate their slain enemy.

What encourages Prabhakaran to violence is that by a series of assassination of rivals—or even potential rivals—the Liberation Tigers of Tamil Eelam (LTTE) have emerged as the sole guerrilla group fighting militarily for an independent Eelam. In the past twenty years, besides killing thousands of innocent non-combatants, the organization has carried out the assassination of a number of moderate politicians who had opposed the LTTE. A feature of LTTE's tactic has been the use of "suicide" bombers, who knowingly detonate bombs carried on their own person, and in the process blow themselves up, taking with them their targeted persons. The 100 per cent record in such assassinations that LTTE had boasted of, has however been dented now. For example, President Chandrika Kumartunga has escaped two such attempts because the suicide bombers could not position themselves, or had detonated prematurely. The LTTE relies on moles within it's victim's circles and the ability to access the target at close quarters. Murder at Prabhakaran's whim, fear, and paranoia is the LTTE's calling card.

LTTE's Infiltration of India: A National Security Threat

The undercurrent of British imperialist promoted "Dravida" secessionists' ideology has been exploited by the LTTE, to propagate the concept of a pan-Tamilian state and obtain collaborators within India.

Secessionism has been an undercurrent feature of Tamil politics in India, induced by British imperialists since the 1930s, when the anti-Brahmin movement led by E.V. Ramaswamy Naicker demanded a separate homeland for "Dravida people," i.e. south Indians living in the Madras Presidency. Brahmins of Tamil Nadu were in the forefront of India's freedom struggle led by Mahatma Gandhi. He founded the Dravida Kazgham (DK) in 1944, which demanded an independent, sovereign and democratic Tamil Republic.

The DK is now run by K. Veeramani as a kind of family trust. His son, based in Chicago (USA), coordinates his foreign activities. DK has been the India-based infrastructural backbone of the LTTE from the very first day. Nine of its prominent members were amongst the 26 sentenced to death by the trial court in the Rajiv Gandhi assassination case. The DK runs a perpetual hate campaign against Brahmins. Once when Jayalalitha was Chief Minister of Tamilnadu it had targeted me once by forging photographs and trying to frame me in bogus cases—probably to please her but more certainly to earn credits with LTTE, and viscerally because the DK considers me a Brahmin who is not afraid of them.

Incidentally, the DK, which does not even have a single member in Delhi (nor anyone there who knows of the organization), was given in 1999 one acre of land next to the Delhi International Airport, as well as the funds to construct a three-story building named Periyar Memorial. This was done at the direction of the Congress-ruled Delhi State government, *and even after the Supreme Court had judged that the LTTE backed by the DK was responsible for carrying out the assassination of Rajiv Gandhi.* In July 2000, I had met Mrs Sonia Gandhi at her residence and had asked her if she had directed Delhi Chief Minister Mrs Shiela Dikshit to provide all these facilities to the DK, and if so why, when the DK had been held, by the Jain Commission, to be the infrastructure to carry out Rajiv Gandhi's assassination. She replied that she was not aware that the DK had been indicted by the Jain Commission! Based on my complaint, however, the Lieutenant Governor of Delhi got the building demolished. I had complained that the DK memorial building was *de facto* a transit camp for the LTTE for them to access the Delhi airport, to enter and exist from India clandestinely.

While the LTTE used Jaffna Tamils for its core and confidential operations, it has a very important logistical network service provided by Indian sympathizers or dupes like P. Nedumaran of the Tamil Desiya Iyakkam (TDI), V. Gopalasamy (*nee* Vaiko) of the MDMK, the PMK, besides of course the "dependable" DK, and certain as yet unidentified "persons in high places." The DMK provides the terrorist outfit the media and local logistical support. But as LTTE operative Athirai, a young girl in her late teens, told the CBI-led SIT, LTTE leadership has contempt for Indian politicians who collaborate with them since they are "so greedy for money." They can "betray" LTTE whenever the organization will be on the run, she said.

The arrest and interrogation of Ravi, alias Ravichandran, and eighteen others in December 1991 revealed attempts by the LTTE to forge militant organizations in Tamil Nadu as well. The complete ramifications of the Tamil National Retrieval Troops (TNRT) and the Tamil National Liberation Army (TNLA) set up in 1987-1988 are not clear. The outfits had been the support base for forest and ivory smuggler Veerappan (see *Hindu,* 18 November 2001). According to press reports, obviously based on police briefing, Ravi claimed that he had been part of the entourage of Kittu, who had headed the LTTE liaison office in Madras. Ravi accompanied him on his return to Jaffna in 1988 and came to the notice of the LTTE intelligence chief Pottu Amman. Ravi was trained in the use of weapons and was motivated to return to India. He was provided money and weapons and given instructions to build up the TNRT by raising cadres to be trained by the LTTE and in more practical terms to build up the LTTE communications network in India. It was Ravi who introduced Sivarasan in Tamil Nadu in November 1990. Following the Rajiv Gandhi assassination, he maintained contact with the LTTE in Jaffna and for a while hid one member of the assassination team, Subha. While all of the India-based TNRT team have been arrested, and jailed, another TNRT team is reported to be in Jaffna and is estimated at one thousand strong.

There have also been reports about links between the LTTE and the People's War Group (PWG) of Maoists. The PWG is the largest and best armed group active in large and poverty-stricken areas of Andhra Pradesh, Maharashtra, Orissa, and Madhya Pradesh. They have been involved in a long, though low-key insurgency against the Indian state in a region that is not only poor, but heavily forested. Marepalli Basavaraju, a functionary of the PWG, who had surrendered, claimed that an LITE explosives expert had trained his group—in laying mines in 1989. The PWG attacks have shown that they know how to lay mines, an ability that the Marxist-Leninist groups did not have earlier.

A nexus between the United Liberation Front of Assam (ULFA) and the LTTE emerged in 1991 from the discovered presence of LTTE training camps in the state. The Chandrashekhar Government's timely dismissal of the Assam Government put an end to the nexus, at least its operational significance. But on 13 December 1997, after presenting his credentials to President K.R. Narayanan, the new Cambodian Ambassador to India, Sim Suong, told the PTI that he concurred with India's then Defence Minister Mulayam Singh Yadav that Khmer Routge was supplying weapons to ULFA, *but added that it was through the LTTE not directly.*

V.P. Singh became the Prime Minister on 2 December 1989, and immediately took three steps that gave the LTTE a tremendous boost in acquiring legitimacy for its activities in India. The first was the decision to convert Rajiv Gandhi's plan of phased de-induction of IPKF from Sri Lanka, to a total and complete withdrawal by March 1990, making it appear that the LTTE was the victorious freedom fighter and the Indian Army, the defeated force of suppression. Second, he asked Karunanidhi to open a dialogue with all the Tamil militant groups for a peaceful settlement amongst themselves, for the stated purpose of participating in the democratic process of devolution of power to the North Eastern Provinces of Sri Lanka, within the broad framework of integrity of Sri Lanka. But there was a catch in that direction to Karunanidhi: that if no solution was reached India would not give any more help to any of the groups, nor allow the Indian mainland to be used for their activities. This ultimatum suited the LTTE, since it was the only group that had by then become independent of Indian support. The catch proviso, in effect, was to crush the rivals to the LTTE. No wonder then that the LTTE remained adamant during their parleys with Karunanidhi: by an insistent demand on the formation of Eelam, something the Central Government could not agree without an international consensus and mandate. Third, V.P. Singh directed Karunanidhi to allow LTTE to bring their injured and maimed to Tamil Nadu hospitals and have them treated. Medicines could also be made available to the LTTE. The LTTE was also facilitated by the petrol/diesel stations set up liberally in Tamil Nadu on Vaiko's recommendation letters.

Given this leeway, Karunanidhi went overboard in his espousal of the LTTE. Senior leaders of LTTE began meeting Karunanidhi regularly, which had a demoralizing effect on the bureaucracy.

The parleys between Chief Minister Karunanidhi and the LTTE further led to the LTTE getting encouragement to operate in Tamil Nadu with impunity, as it was perceived by officials that the Chief Minister was sympathetic to them and thus gave the implicit signal to them that government machinery ought to cooperate with them. That was the general perception in the state during 1989-90 on the eve of my becoming Union Cabinet Minister for Law and Justice.

The period 1989-90 was the high point in indulging the LTTE militants on Indian soil, and in tolerating their wide ranging criminal and anti-national activities even at the cost of deterioration of the general law and order situation in Tamil Nadu. The State law enforcement machinery had become apathetic and ineffective to face the growing aggressiveness of the LTTE in the State. LTTE arms smuggling, abduction of Indian citizens for purposes of extortion, kidnapping of customs officials, and intimidation of the law enforcing machinery were now tolerated. Officials looked the other way. Jocularly, the Tamil Nadu police called Prabhakaran, the "son-in-law" of Karunanidhi. As early as 30 January 1990, the senior Additional Director of the Intelligence Bureau, Dr. K.V.H. Padmanabhan, sent a note to the PMO [IBU.O.NO.I(14)/90(11) appended here] stating that the LTTE had set up a "rocket propelled hand grenade factory in Coimbatore since August 1989 which grenades were used for killing Indian army jawans of the IPKF!"

The boycott by Karunanidhi, as Chief Minister, of the ceremony to receive the IPKF contingent de-inducted from Sri Lanka was another unpatriotic gimmick of his that was hailed by the LTTE. In fact, the "ouster" of IPKF was celebrated by the LTTE in Sri Lanka like V-day was in London in 1945.

Added to all this, the policy of the Government of Tamil Nadu and the Central Government (headed by V.P. Singh) to allow the

4/(V3)/88(23)

SECRET

INTELLIGENCE BUREAU
(Ministry of Home Affairs)

Subject: SRI LANKAN TAMIL ISSUE - IMPACT ON TAMIL NADU.

With the dead-line set for the deinduction of IPKF by March 31, 1990, and little prospect of agreement among the Eelam groups over the issue of laying down arms causing apprehensions of civil disorder, the rate of refugee influx into Tamil Nadu has been steadily on the rise with 179 arrivals from the island in October 1989, 250 in November and 1,057 in December. 477 refugee families consisting of 834 members mostly from Talai Mannar and Jaffna areas have reached Tamil Nadu this year so far. Official figures confirm the presence of 1007 Sri Lankan Tamil families consisting of 2314 members at Mandapam refugee camp (Ramnad Distt.). There is reason for further [illegible] with reports that another 4,000 Tamil families have been [illegible] at the northern port of Kankesanthurai (Sri Lanka) on their way to Tamil Nadu.

2. While no large scale movement of non-LTTE cadres from Sri Lanka to Tamil Nadu has been noticed, small groups of EPRLF, ENDLF and TELO fleeing from the attacks of LTTE have landed in Tamil Nadu during January, 1990. Some ENDLF cadres (31) had got themselves registered also at Mandapam refugee camp. Some of the groups like the ENDLF have transferred their weapons to Tamil Nadu for future use against their adversaries. On January 29, one such arms cache with 88 AK 47 assault rifles, 64 9mm pistols, 40 LMGs and large quantities of ammunition and other spares was unearthed in the coastal area of Ramanathapuram district under P.S. Uchipuli. Again on January 25 night, the Rameswaram police (Pamban P.S.) had effected some more recovery of ammunition. Earlier on January 23, the Tamil Nadu CID recovered a highly sophisticated powerful Japan-made trans-receiver set with automatic tuner antenna from a private house hired by ENDLF cadres in Tangachimadam (Ramnad).

3. Meanwhile, the LTTE has been taking full advantage of the sympathetic attitude of the ruling DMK in Tamil Nadu. A [illegible] spurt in LTTE activities is seen coinciding with the initiative taken by the Chief Minister of Tamil Nadu in resolving the ethnic issue and holding parleys with the LTTE leadership (A Balasingham and Yogi). Suggestions that all Tamil groups including LTTE should lay down arms and sit together for talks to reach a consensus have not been reportedly relished by the LTTE leaders. Meanwhile, the LTTE militant wing has stepped up its clandestine activities in the State. The LTTE is now maintaining a tri-weekly illicit boat traffic between Velvettithurai (Jaffna district of Sri Lanka) and Mallipatnam (Thanjavur district of Tamil Nadu). The traffic involves transport of medicine, foodstuffs, arms/ammunition. Besides, wounded persons are also brought to Tamil Nadu from time to time for treatment. The group has also [illegible] Chinnamanai (Thanjavur district)

4. Local DMK leaders in the coastal regions of Thanjavur have also been collaborating with LTTE in its illegal traffic in the hinterland. There is also a move on the part of LTTE to open a regular office for its political wing, the Peoples' Liberation Front for Eelam Tamils (PLFT), in Tamil Nadu with the blessings of its patron V. Gopalaswamy, MP (DMK), and the Chief Minister. While the State Police is under constraints to act firmly against the LTTE's illegal activities the Customs personnel in the State are a demoralised lot after the abduction of a Customs patrol in December last and their subsequent release at the intervention of the DMK higher ups with the LTTE. The LTTE has revived its unit for the manufacture of rocket-propelled grenades at Coimbatore and called for 2000 such grenades a week ago reportedly for use againt the IPKF engaged in de-induction. The presence of the fabrication unit came to notice in August 1989 when the Police raided a workshop at Coimbatore manufacturing components for the RPG and arrested four local collaborators including a prominent DK leader.

5. In the ongoing parleys with the Tamil Nadu Chief Minister, the representatives of the non-LTTE groups have felt unhappy at his pro-LTTE instance and have approached other parties like the TMCC-I AIADMK and others to urge the Govt. of India to convene a meeting of all Eelam groups. Speaking at Madras on January 24, Rajiv Gandhi insinuated that Karunanidhi while professing to be champion of Tamil rights had abandoned Tamil interests in Sri Lanka. He welcomed the idea of an all party meeting to decide the Sri Lankan Tamil issue.

(Dr. K.V.H. Padmanabhan)
Sr. Additional Director

H.M.

Principal Secy. to P.M.	:	(Shri B.G. Deshmukh)
Cabinet Secretary	:	(Shri V.C. Pande)
Home Secretary	:	(Shri Shiromani Sharma)
Foreign Secretary	:	(Shri S.K. Singh)
Defence Secretary	:	(Shri Naresh Chandra)
Secretary (R), Cab. Sectt.	:	(Shri A.K. Verma)

injured LTTE cadres to come into India for treatment (even while the IPKF was fighting the LTTE), enabled the LTTE to further consolidate its network in India. The Jain Commission's Interim Report (page 941, para 73.23) contains the secret correspondence between V.P. Singh and Karunanidhi on this subject. On page 943, para 73.20, there is also a description of how the LTTE used its Tamil Nadu bases to train ULFA with the knowledge of the Chief Minister.

The Indian Peace Keeping Force (IPKF) confronted the LTTE in a campaign which left altogether nearly 12,000 persons dead and over 5,000 wounded. In this period, the LTTE showed themselves to be tenacious and innovative guerilla fighters. As casualties increased, democratic India failed to respond. The IPKF had to withdraw in March 1990, and this boosted the LTTE's prestige from the propaganda that they had defeated the world's third largest army. The fact is that the IPKF had to fight with one arm tied behind its back, and yet in fact had subdued the LTTE. But the internal sabotage by the DMK and the perfidy of the V.P. Singh government, made the IPKF leave with a job half-done.

LTTE's International Operations

The LTTE raises a part of its funds from an international network of sympathizers and contacts, who are almost invariably Tamils, more especially the Jaffna Tamil diaspora. This network is used to make monthly collections from the overseas Sri Lanka Tamils, an operation that borders on scientific extortion. Tamils are made to fill out forms and bank transfers are effected. Internet banking is nowadays in vogue with the LITE.

The LTTE functions at four distinct levels: (1) publicity and propaganda; (2) arms procurement; (3) modern communications; and (4) fund-raising. The networks overlap to some extent, but command-wise they remain separate. The international propagandist of the LTTE for a long period was Lawrence Thilakar, a Jaffna-born Tamil and a graduate of Jaffna University, who joined the movement in the early 1980s. There are reports that he had lost reputation inside the organization, and due to corruption charges, has now been replaced. The "International Secretariat" of the LTTE has certainly shifted to London at 211, Katherine Road, London E6 IBU (Telephone: 44-20-8503-4294), and is probably supervised by Balasingham, the LTTE ideologue. He too now seems, according to media reports, terminally ill with cancer.

Thilakar had operated overground from an LTTE office in a Paris apartment at the apex of an organization that comprises 38 offices globally. About four million dollars a month are debited into the LTTE numbered accounts. Aside from Western states with large Tamil communities, the "Tigers" are represented in countries as far-flung as Norway and Botswana. The LTTE also works through sympathetic umbrella groups such as the Australasian Federation of Tamil Associations and the Federation of Associations of Canadian Tamils, and the World Tamil Organization.

The LTTE puts out videos projecting in detail the results of government air strikes. And it uses the Internet both as a propaganda tool and as a means to appeal for funds.

The LTTE organizer for procurement of international weapons and its financial collaterals is K. Selvarajan Pathmanathan, an inconspicuous man of medium height and build. The 41-year-old Tamil, known as "KP," carries several passports, changes names frequently, and has access to multiple bank accounts across the globe. He is also reputed to have an impressive facility for forging documents. According to a reliable source, "KP" was in India a few days before and after Rajiv Gandhi's assassination, probably to assess how his work would be affected internationally by the assassination. He is reported to have left from Mumbai on 26 May 1991.

"KP" works as the head of a team that has the crucial job of supplying LTTE with the hardware to wage war. The CBI/SIT has prepared a thorough dossier on him.

According to a well-researched article in *Asiaweek* magazine (26 July 1996), Anthony Davis states that "KP" is often sighted in Pnom Penh, Phuket and Bangkok. He might have negotiated a shipment of Chinese rocket-launchers with a friendly Australian arms dealer in Hong Kong. On any day, he could be discussing the price of "silence" with a Thai customs official in a Phuket restaurant.

Principally, he had been headquartered in Hong Kong. Some intelligence inputs suggests that he has moved to Macao. However, with his presence coming to the adverse notice of the Chinese authorities since the island merged politically with the mainland in July 1997, "KP" is rumoured to have "retired" and is said to be grooming a successor to humour Prabhakaran. Whether any one can step into his shoes ought to be a cause for Prabhakaran's worry, especially since US, Canada, Singapore and Hong Kong have decided to regard the LTTE formally as a terrorist organization. Australia, U.K. and France cannot remain outside this growing consensus for long. The US Federal Bureau of Investigation, which has set up a New Delhi office, has been tasked to track down the LTTE network in South Asia, especially its cash spinning narcotics activity. In September 2006, the FBI raided the houses of several Sri Lankan Tamil residents in the US and arrested about ten persons on the charge of raising funds for the LTTE through the Tamil Rehabilitation Organization [TRO]. The TRO was claiming to raise funds for the people affected by the Tsunami disaster. Similar raids have been effected by the Australian police in Sydney, Perth and Melbourne.

Prabhakaran may soon find the world is closing in on him, especially since the US security organizations have identified the LTTE as a terrorist outfit that is posing "maximum threat" and the EU is complying with this description.

Drawing on the resources of 450,000 members of a global Tamil diaspora, KP's network links commercial companies and small businesses, informal banking channels, a fleet of ships, political offices, aid and human rights organizations, arms dealers and foreign mecenaries.

The LTTE arms-procurement underground network is, however, naturally shrouded in the deepest secrecy. The network has been painstakingly built up since 1983 and is worth millions of dollars. At the apex, its headquarters is at Velvattithurai, a fishing port on the north coast of the Jaffna peninsula. Based on a detailed CBI/SIT report on "KP" now accessible through Parliament Library the following aspects of KP's operations are worthy of notice.

"KP" began his work as LTTE's agent by specializing in document forging and in opening up LTTE's international network. In 1984, he organized one of LTTE's early weapons purchases with an Australian arms dealer. Early shipments on chartered ships were run to India and from there moved in speed boats across the Palk Strait to Jaffna or the northeast coast.

Between 1985 and 1989, the LTTE phased out deployment of chartered vessels allegedly with the help of Ms Pratima Das, an elusive Mumbai resident, and began to buy its own ocean-going vessels. The fleet—which today numbers five or six small freighters—was registered under Panamanian, Honduran or Liberian flags, crewed often by Velvattithurai Tamils, and owned by various front companies. Illicit cargo ferrying has become LTTE's global business, conducting drugs-for-weapons transactions. [*The Hindu,* 27-29 March 2000 appended here.]

By the early 1990s, "KP" had substantially diversified the LTTE's arms network. In the early days, LTTE relied on West Asian and European dealers—with end-user certificates often obtained from pliable Nigerian officials. But since 1994 it has extended its reach to cover South-East Asia and Pakistan's booming Afghan arms bazaar. LTTE operatives appear to have had no problems operating in Pakistan. Islamabad's security services, the ISI, has assisted it because any enemy of India is a friend of Pakistan.

'Shipping profits funded LTTE war machine'

By V.S. Sambandan

COLOMBO, 26 MARCH. The Liberation Tigers of Tamil Eelam (LTTE), has reportedly established a "shipping base on a Thai island near the holiday resort of Phuket."

Assembling what it termed as "an intricate jigsaw" of the Tigers' shipping operations, the leading international shipping publication, *Lloyd's List,* has said the LTTE's shipping operations fetched for the group "colossal profits" which funded its "war machine."

The report, which was published in today's *Sunday Island,* said the LTTE's earlier base "in the Myanmar island of Tawante had been vacated in January 1996 following diplomatic pressure on Rangoon from Colombo."

Describing the LTTE as "one of the world's unusual shipowners," the report said its "flags of convenience vessels spend much of their time on legitimate commercial work" but "their real purpose is to provide logistical capability to fuel" the separatist conflict.

Most of the LTTE's vessels were registered in Panama, Honduras or Liberia and were owned through front companies headed by Mr. K. Pathmanathan, the report said, adding that the crew members "usually from Velvattithurai in the Jaffna peninsula (the birthplace of LTTE chief, Mr. V. Prabhakaran) are paid for their work, unless they are Tiger cadres."

The report also said that the deadly consignments brought in by the Tigers included 50 tonnes of TNT and 10 tonnes of RDX explosives from the Ukrainian Black Sea port, Nikalayev.

The RDX, it is reported, was used by the Tigers in the January 1996 truck bomb explosion that devastated

Colombo's financial centre, killing 91 persons and injuring over 1,400.

Yet another major heist was in 1997 when one of the LTTE's ships, posing as a commercial liner, picked up 32,000 mortar shells manufactured by the Zimbabwe Defence Industries and ordered by the Sri Lankan Government.

"They simply sent one of their vessels to the Mozambique port of Beira and were able to pick up the consignment by pretending she (the vessel) was acting for the Sri Lankan authorities.

The bombs were later used against the Government forces," the report said.

Among the setbacks suffered by the Tigers' shipping network was the sinking of the *m.v. Ahat,* which was intercepted by Indian naval authorities off the Tamil Nadu coast in 1993.

The ship was sunk after one of the LTTE's leaders, Sathasivam Krishnakumar, alias Kittu, who was on board the vessel, ordered it to be blown up.

Yet another major reversal was when one of its vessels was sunk off Trincomalee in 1996 when it was offloading a "large consignment of weapons," the report said.

The Hindu, Monday, 27 March 2000

LTTE's flourishing shipping network

By V. Jayanth

The publication by the 'Lloyds's List' of the Liberation Tigers of Tamil Eelam's (LTTE) profitable and strategic shipping operations out of Southeast Asia, may at best be a documentation of a well-known network.

The LTTE has been functioning out of different parts of Southeast Asia for over a decade now. It provided a ready platform to shift most of its operations after India signed the Indo-Sri Lanka Agreement in 1987.

Analysts and police sources tracking the LTTE operations say "Singapore was the first choice of the Tamil Tigers, but they also realised that operating out of that City State involved a lot of restraint and regulations. But in 1992-93, the Singapore Government cracked down on the LTTE and it was forced to shift the bulk of its operations to other centres."

Apparently, the Tamil Tigers found a congenial setting in both Myanmar and Thailand. The availability of a number of tiny islands between these two countries, some of them uninhabited, provided a convenient base for the LTTE to function.

The sources explain that Mr. K. Pathmanathan (better known as KP) enjoyed such a 'clout' in the region that he managed to put together a fleet of small and medium vessels. They were mostly registered in Latin America and the nearby islands, but operated out of Bangkok. Quite often, they were refurbished and re-registered in Thailand to avoid detection or familiarity.

Initially, the LTTE preferred a tie-up with the military junta in Myanmar and made use of the country's port as well as islands for its trade and transshipment. Following reports from that region, the Sri Lankan Government took it up with Yangon, which must have conveyed its own message to the LTTE.

That was also the period when the Tamil Tigers were smuggling in a lot of weapons from the former Soviet Union States and procuring some from Cambodia and Thailand. The group had close links to the Khmer Rouge, the Cambodian army and the Government in Phnom Penh. It bought arms and ammunition from all three channels, because all of them were facing a resource crunch. The visa-on-arrival facility, the high level of corruption and the French connection that Cambodia provided were all advantageous to the Tamil Tigers.

When Myanmar applied some pressure on the LTTE to move out of its territory, the Tigers took refuge in small islands off Thailand, near Phuket. This provided a much more convenient link, because Phuket also had a fairly well-connected airport.

The Sri Lankan Government has been frequently taking up this issue with both Myanmar and Thailand, besides briefing the Governments of Singapore and Malaysia.

Sources say "except for financial transactions, the LTTE does not want to register its presence in Singapore. It faces hostility in Kuala Lumpur and the Malaysian Government has consistently put down all forms of pro-LTTE activity there."

According to analysts, a base in Southeast Asia offers several advantages to the LTTE. Given the extensive network of Sri Lankan Tamils living abroad, thousands of them becoming economic refugees, a lot of funds are also being collected around the world—from Canada and Australia to South Africa, Europe and the U.K.

Channeling these funds, providing logistic support to the LTTE in eastern Sri Lanka and earning some profits out of the fleet of vessels that its 'front' organisation owns, have been some of the tasks assigned to 'KP.' But intelligence sources believe that Mr. Pathmanathan has "retired" and installed a deputy in his place to take charge of the shipping operations. He continues to "advice and guide." There was an interesting experience for the State Trading Corporation (STC) a couple of years ago. One of its shipments of rice went "missing" in Southeast Asia. The ship itself could not be traced. Finally, an advertisement in a Singapore paper of an auction of rice led to the unravelling of the mystery. A refurbished ship from Bangkok was caught with the rice and impounded.

As the Sri Lankan Government must have realised by now, it may be difficult to contain the LTTE's operations globally. Some of its commercial activities may even be legal and very profitable and the host Government may not be able to halt them. Unless there is evidence to show that these agencies are linked to the LTTE or carry on illegal, contraband trade, it becomes difficult to crack down on such operations. The same may be true about the fund-raising activities of the LTTE, because they are ostensibly meant to help refugees seeking a new lease of life.

News, 29 March 2000

An important LTTE cell was established in the Thai town of Trang (*Indian Express*, 27 March 2000) before it was shifted north to a front company in Phuket. Deals with global arms dealers were put together in Hong Kong, while Singapore became the favoured market for the purchase of "dual-use" items such as computers, electronic goods, outboard motors and diving gear.

LTTE vessels are believed to have begun shipping timber from Myanmar to Thailand in the late 1980s, a line of business that soon brought them into contact with the Myanmar (Burma) military. Some time after mid-1990, the contacts resulted in the establishment of an LTTE base at the small town of Twantay, in the Irrawaddy delta south of Yangon (Rangoon). Narcotics running, in which the LTTE now has a dubious fame for its "reliability," came useful in Burma. However, it is now clear that the LTTE has given up its lucrative Burma base, and it has moved to two other more developed port towns: Phuket in Thailand and Karachi in Pakistan.

According to intelligence sources, Norwegian mercenaries assisted in the training of LTTE frogmen in underwater demolition techniques. Yet today, Norway is being asked to mediate between the Sri Lankan Government and the LTTE!

Gaining an effective anti-aircraft capability—specifically, in surface-to-air missiles—was a priority LTTE pursuit. LTTE personnel had training in the use of SAMs, courtesy an RAW course in 1985. But India did not release any missiles to its erstwhile "protege." LTTE's efforts to acquire Stinger missiles from the Afghan war leftovers did not bear fruit but in 1994, "KP" was able to get his hands on Soviet made SA-7s. The missiles are believed to have been sold by corrupt Cambodian generals and transported across the Thai border in late 1994. The weapons reached the Sri Lanka coast well before the LTTE resumed hostilities on the island in April 1995. The SA-7s were used to down two aging Avro transport planes of the Sri Lanka government.

An LTTE vessel later identified as *M.V. Swanee,* left the Ukrainian Black Sea port of Mikolayev. In August 1995, a Dhaka front company, Carlton Trading, gave the LTTE the end-user certificate, purportedly signed by Bangladesh's Secretary for Defence, that indicated its military as the approved recipient. Thereby the LTTE imported 50 tons of TNT and 10 tons of RDX explosives. The M.V. *Swanee,* with the cargo, left the Black Sea port of Milkdayer in Ukraine, and it arrived off the northeastern Sri Lanka coast in September, having called at Twantay en route. As per LTTE practice, the ship had by that time a different name. Protected by Sea Tiger speed boats, its deadly cargo was off-loaded and transferred to several jungle bases. Some of the Ukrainian RDX was put to horrific use on 31 January 1996; a truck bomb exploded outside the Central Bank building in Colombo killing 91 and injuring over 1,400. It was one of the most devastating terrorist attacks in history.

Sathasivam Krishnakumar, *alias* Kittu, the LTTE chief of Jaffna, had lost a leg in an as yet unexplained ambush in March 1987. Thereafter, he was asked to head the Madras office of the outfit where he cultivated political leaders and maintained links with intelligence officials and oversaw the LTTE network around the world. In fact, as a Minister I was shocked to learn from RAW officials after the Rajiv Gandhi assassination, that Kittu was considered to be our mole, and he had received regular payments for it! For a year after the IPKF-LTTE hostilities began, Kittu was allowed to remain free and was arrested in Chennai only in mid-1980; he was actually allowed to go to Jaffna, from where he disappeared. Kittu later ran the London office of the LTTE and after his expulsion in 1991 he ran the show of shipping weapons to Jaffna from Geneva. But improved intelligence work and stepped-up Indian and Sri Lankan naval patrols during Narasimha Rao's tenure as Prime Minister cost the LTTE several ocean going vessels. One was the *M.V. Yahata,* which left Phuket with a huge weapons cargo loaded on to the ship by the Pakistan Navy under ISI supervision in Karachi in January 1993. On board the *Yahata*—along with a shipment of arms and explosives—was London-based Krishnakumar Sathasivam (better known as "Kittu"), the former LTTE Jaffna commander and a close Prabhakaran associate. In the Bay of Bengal, the *M.V. Yahata* became *M.V. Ahat* by painting over the first and last letters in the ship's name. His end came on 15 January 1993 when the Indian Navy patrolling the sea southeast of Madras came across the four-hundred-tonne ship, the *M.V. Yahata, alias Ahat,* without navigation lights, en route to the Madras port for inspection! Kittu, who was on board, ordered the LTTE cadre to commit suicide and the ship was set on fire and destroyed. Crew members who had been asked to jump overboard were arrested. They provided details of the incident as well as confirming that the ship had been carrying nearly 25,000 litres of petrol as well as arms and explosives.

The biggest LTTE maritime disaster, however, occurred in 1996. A shipment of weapons, ammunition and explosives believed to have been purchased from Cambodia worth several million dollars, left the port of Phuket in early February 1996 aboard the freighter *Comex-Joux 3.* At sea, in line with standard LTTE procedure, the vessel changed its name to *Horizon.* But a tip from Western sources in Thailand had already blown the game. On its journey across the-Bay of Bengal, the freighter was tracked by the Indian Navy and Orissa-based spy planes of the Aviation Research Centre, a RAW sister organization. It was intercepted by Indian naval vessels off Sri Lanka's east coast. On 14 February 1996, as the Indians stood guard, Sri Lanka Pucc'ara attack fighters and patrol boats moved in for the kill.

Since the UPA Government coming to power in Delhi with pro-LTTE Indian politicians as Ministers, the vigilance displayed during the previous governments since 1991 has gone. While the Indian establishment does not favour Eelam, the LTTE makes do with the subversion of India's national interests by these Indian Ministers. Replacing the munitions, and maintaining the LTTE war machine now in the field, cannot any more hinge on funds raised from the international Tamil disapora. With the loss of the substantial Jaffna population, and an eroding taxation base on the Jaffna peninsula, the LTTE's international funding tactics is today more crucial for its survival than ever. Like all terrorist organizations, the LTTE is now depending more and more on narcotics trade for financing its weapon procurement. But in that may lie the seeds of its destruction, since the international alertness on drug trafficking is much greater than for extortion of money from a diaspora. Perhaps the greatest error, committed by LTTE, after Rajiv Gandhi's assassination, is its linking up with the Pakistani drug mafia and the ISI.

Hard evidence implicating the LTTE and its leadership in narcotics is slowly spilling out (*Times of India,* 2 October 2000). In the late 1980s, Tamil expatriates and asylum seekers emerged as movers of Afghan and Pakistan heroin via India and West Asia to Europe. Many were arrested and jailed, notably in Italy, and many had contacts with the LTTE. Indeed, one former militant had told *Asiaweek* that his first arms-buying visit to Pakistan in 1984 had been in the company of Tamil heroin smugglers.

The Tactics of the LTTE with Tamil Diaspora

Of the 38 offices of LTTE located worldwide, the most modern and least publicized is its office in Palermo, Sicily, in Italy. The LTTE in-house journal from the Palermo office is more glossy and professionally brought out than that of any other organization in Italy. Palermo is known as an important terminus for international narcotics trafficking and of the Mafia. The European Commission's envoy to South Asia in 1996 confirmed LTTE's link with the Mafia. As the term "narco-terrorism" has become prevalent, the LTTE needs cash to pay for weapons. Narcotics trade is the most cash-spinning business in the world today for the reliable "runners" like the LTTE. The LTTE provides the best runners in that sinister line.

But less well known is the LTTE's involvement in antique smuggling from Tamil Nadu mostly to Europe. Priceless Chola period statues, wantonly and for corrupt motives, declared as non-antiques by the Human Resources Development Ministry have been taken out of India.

Today Canada among Western nations has the single largest concentration of Sri Lankan Tamils which had led the LTTE to establish an active base in Canada for its overseas propaganda as well as fund-raising activity. Within Canada itself there were many complaints of coercion and intimidatory tactics beings adopted by the LTTE in collecting money from Tamils. The "Tigers" openly issued receipts for large donations. These receipts had on them the emblem of the LTTE and an embossed signature of the LTTE supremo Velupillai Prabhakaran. Receipts for large amounts had the signature of the LTTE chief in Canada on them. People were asked to contribute to the LTTE or its front organizations, such as the Tamil Rehabilitation Organization. When people tried to contribute to organizations such as the Red Cross, they were dissuaded from doing so.

Soon enough, the Canadian Government got alerted by the coercive activities of the LTTE. It refused to grant a visa to Lawrence Thilagar, spokesman and acting secretary-general of the LTTE's International Secretariat, to visit Canada, signaling a change of attitude in 1997.

The next anti-LTTE signal came when Suresh Manickavasagam, the chief of the LTTE in Canada, and fund collector for the LTTE Front, the WTM, was arrested on the basis of a national security certificate of 18 October 1995. He had come as a refugee in 1991. He was detained pending deportation under this certificate, which was jointly signed by the Canadian. Minister of Immigration and the Solicitor-General. The import of the certificate was that Suresh belonged to a class of persons who were considered a security threat to Canada and were therefore *persona non grata* in that country. In Suresh's case, they related to his alleged involvement in terrorism, his having been a member of a terrorist organization and his membership of an organization that engages in and is likely to engage in terrorism. The organization cited was the LTTE, which Canada banned as a terrorist organization on 6 December 1998. Suresh appealed for a judicial review of the executive order. On 29 August 1998, a Federal Court Judge, Max Teitelbaum, heard the case in Toronto and held that the order issued against the LTTE chief was reasonable and valid.

The LTTE in Canada then spent a lot of money to mount a legal defence. Leading Canadian lawyers like Barbara Jackmann were retained and a galaxy of witnesses assembled. After lengthy proceedings, the Federal. Court of Appeals Judge, Joseph Robertson, on 21 January 2000, dismissed the LTTE's appeal on behalf of Suresh. Justice Robertson observed that the LTTE was "a terrorist organization that believes in killing innocent persons." A damning judgement indeed! But more damaging was the Judge's opinion that even if Suresh risked torture upon deportation and arrival in Colombo the balance of human rights for terrorists in Canada is in favour of deportation!

The Canadian authorities are now extremely concerned about a Tamil Nadu connection in the LTTE's fund-raising activity. Last year, the Canadian branch of the LTTE, the World Tamil Movement, held its 10th anniversary celebrations in Toronto. Political figures from Tamil Nadu, including P. Nedumaran, Dr. S. Ramadoss, Theeran, and R. Janarthanam, were present at a gathering of over 15,000 Tamils. Vast amounts of money were collected at that meeting. How much the Indian supporters of LTTE, invoking Prabhakaran's name received, is to be found out.

Ironically, the very same LTTE which utilizes Tamil Nadu personalities to help fill its coffers can also ruthlessly sabotage performances by inconvenient or independent Indian artists. When cine idol Rajnikant and his wife Latha embarked on a tour of Europe and Canada three years ago, they found the LTTE quite hostile. The "Tigers" engaged in a systematic hate propaganda against Rajnikant and intimidated people into not attending the Rajnikant shows. Two of the three shows in Canada were cancelled while one was marked by poor attendance.

The reason for the "Tigers" sabotaging the Rajnikant shows was that they were organized by those who did not have the "approval" of the LTTE. Other shows by lesser-known Indian artists too have been undermined by the LTTE in Western countries, including Canada. Nor does the LTTE favour a free Press even abroad.

"It is with a sense of deep regret that I am forced to make the announcement that *Muncharie* [the Toronto-based Tamil weekly], is ceasing publication from today. Circumstances beyond our control have compelled us to suspend publication and the reason is public knowledge as far as the Canadian Tamil community is concerned." Thus bade farewell D.B.S. Jeyaraj, a respected Sri Lankan Tamil journalist, a former Nieman Fellow at Harvard working over the years to provide balanced perspective on Sri Lankan affairs. His Tamil weekly, *Muncharie,* started in Toronto in June 1993, became a successful magazine. In April 1996, however, the publication was forced to close down. This was the result of a systematic, mafia-style campaign conducted by the LTTE.

Muncharie had been penalized by the Canadian World Tamil Movement (WTM), a front organization of the Liberation Tigers of Tamil Eelam, for the "offense" of adhering faithfully to the dictum: "Comment is free, but facts are sacred."

In 1993, Jeyaraj was assaulted by a gang of four Tamil youths outside the Ontario Science Centre. They accused him of writing against the LTTE. Using rods and baseball bats, they broke his leg. He also received head injuries. Thereafter, he received an ominous telephone call from Lawrence Thilakar, the international spokesman of the LTTE, in Paris. Taking umbrage at news-items in *Muncharie,* he accused Jeyaraj of working against the LTTE and labelled him a "traitor."

When Chandrika Kumaratunga became President of Sri Lanka, *Muncharie* welcomed her victory, and urged the LTTE to grasp the hand of friendship extended by her and resolve the problem through dialogue and discussion. The "Tigers," however, did not like it one bit.

In April, 1995, Mariathasan, the LTTE representative in Montreal, turned up at Jeyaraj's home unexpectedly with a mutual friend. He said that he had returned from Sri Lanka after a prolonged stay. He claimed that he had met the LTTE chief, Prabhakaran, and had a lengthy discussion about the Canadian situation. Mariathasan said that Prabhakaran had told him that he was unhappy about some of Jeyaraj's writings. "Don't lose the regard the leader has for you," said Mariathasan, ominously.

Jeyaraj told his wife that by following an independent editorial line he had aroused the wrath of the "Tigers." "They are so powerful that they can prevent our paper functioning," he told her. "If that happens, let us shut down the paper. It is better to do that rather than compromise and feel guilty about it," she replied.

The number of anonymous calls began to increase. Some calls were amusing. One call warned: "If 5 soldiers are killed write 50 were killed. If 5 'Tigers' are killed write '0.05 Tigers were killed'." This was the new arithmetic that the LTTE propagated brazenly in its website, tamiltigers.com.

Soon it became clear that Jeyaraj was not going to change. So the LTTE approach changed. A vicious and systematic campaign was launched targeting Tamil shopkeepers selling *Muncharie.* Young men, mainly students, began visiting Tamil shops and began urging them not to sell *Muncharie.* Telephone calls were made and some callers identified themselves. Faxes stating that "Muncharie will not be sold here" were sent to some shops. One shopkeeper was told that they would plant heroin on him if he sold the weekly. From information supplied by some brave shopkeepers, some of these persons were identified. Some were members of a local Tamil gang considered close to the Tigers; some were WTM volunteers from the local area; others were students belonging to the Student Wing of the WTM. In many instances, the students were from educational institutions outside the Metro Toronto region. Unfortunately, those who gave information were reluctant to complain publicly to the police for fear of the Tigers.

Another subtle campaign was afoot. The treasurer of the WTM, Ranja Rasa Kandiah, along with his brother-in-law operated an import business. These persons supply to many shops and also provide them with substantial credit. This served as leverage when some of the shops were asked to sabotage *Muncharie* sales. These shops would thereafter hide *Muncharie* and then return copies saying, "No sale."

Matters came to a head in December 1995 when shops were told explicitly that *Muncharie* had been "banned." In a disturbing development, the persons who distributed the paper to the shops were threatened over the telephone.

One evening in December 1995, a gang of Tamils went in vehicles to several Tamil shops in Toronto. They unleashed a spree of violence against shopkeepers and took away the newspapers by force. Letters were sent out by post to advertisers, asking them to stop advertising. Telephone calls were made in the same fashion. "Friendly persuasion" was conducted through third parties. One by one the advertisers succumbed: they began cancelling their advertisements. The *Muncharie* was a 40-page tabloid with some 18 pages of advertisements; but soon the paper came down to 24 pages with only two pages of advertisements. In this situation, *Muncharie* began losing money. *Muncharie,* once a Tamil immigrant success story in Canada, was sliding fast into debt and ruin.

In an interview, Jeyaraj told *Frontline* (31 May 1996): "The WTM, which claims to fight for the freedom of Tamils, suppressed the freedom of expression of a Tamil newspaper. Ironically, this has happened not in the Tiger-controlled areas of Sri Lanka but in the democratic state of Canada."

So after a hectic phase of journalism, *Muncharie* bade farewell. A ruthless fascist organization had used its formidable manpower to crush a small Tamil weekly. The LTTE had stifled *Muncharie* because Canada's Tamil readers believed *Muncharie* more than the propaganda churned out by the LTTE. This had drastically affected their fund-raising activities in Canada. The Royal Canadian Mountain Police have since confirmed the syndrome exposed by Jeyaraj.

By now, in the year 2006, the LTTE having emerged as the largest of the Tamil fighting groups, possesses an extensive array of communication systems that gives it a tremendous "force multiplier" in fighting the Sri Lankan armed forces.

At the height of its presence in Tamil Nadu in 1989-90, the LTTE's Communications Centre was located near Thanjavur, in Tamil Nadu state in south-eastern India, and just 140 km north-west of Jaffna. Another important LTTE communications station, equipped with "high powered transmitters" and "interception" facilities, was located at Vedaranayam, on the extreme south-eastern tip of India, just across the Palk Strait from Jaffna. Other communications centres were located at Nagappattinam, the LTTE's main military base near the Nallur Kovil on the north-west outskirts of Jaffna, and at the LTTE bases at Mannar, Kilinochchi, Mulatlvu, Vavuniya and Batticaloa in the north and east of Sri Lanka. These stations were in constant radio communication, using high-powered HF transmitters.

During 1988-91, the LTTE's training and logistic support bases in Tamil Nadu were linked by a sophisticated wireless network. The bases were located at Madras, Coimbatore, Periyar (Erode), Salem, Dharmapuri, Tiruchi, Thanjavur, Pudukkottai, Madurai, and Ramanathapuram. Short-range FM radio was used to connect these bases to the HF trunk system. It was only after the dismissal of the DMK Ministry in 1991 that much of this network was disabled! Since 1998, the LTTE communications network has once again begun to revive and spread.

In Sri Lanka Citizens band (CB) radios and walkie-talkies are used for field communications. For example, every area commander and some of Prabhakaran's trusted men were provided with walkie-talkies, and they were in constant touch with their main base (near the Nallur Kovil) and the headquarters in Jaffna.

LTTE communications are monitored by both Sri Lankan and Indian agencies. The coverage includes communications between LTTE bases in Sri Lanka and Tamil Nadu state and between LTTE bases and groups within Sri Lanka; and it includes communications concerning logistic support, attack plans and battlefield operations.

At least five Indian agencies also monitor LTTE communications—the Electronic Technical Section (ETS) of the Research and Analysis Wing (RAW) of the Cabinet Secretariat in New Delhi; the Intelligence Bureau (IB) of the Ministry of Home Affairs; the Signals Intelligence Directorate (SID) of the Military Intelligence Directorate of the Indian Army; Army signals units serving with the IPKF in Sri Lanka; and Q Branch of the Tamil Nadu Police in Madras.

In Tamil Nadu state, for example, both Indian Central (i.e. RAW, SID and IB) and State (i.e. Q Branch of the Tamil Nadu Police) agencies monitor LTTE communications.

Radio monitoring provided the IPKF with valuable intelligence concerning the political and strategic intentions, plans and preparations of the LTTE. During the third quarter of 1988, for example, when an important IPKF monitored round of surrender negotiations was being completed between the Sri Lankan Government and the LTTE (and which provided for the total disarmament of the LTTE), intercepts of LTTE wireless communications revealed its plans for buying weapons (oiled and greased and placed in polythene bags) for later recovery. That is, the LTTE was caught cheating.

Monitoring of LTTE radio communications had frequently provided the IPKF with indications and warning of LTTE operations as plans and preparations were often reported and discussed on radio nets.

According to Lt. Gen. Sardeshpande, IPKF chief before its withdrawal in March 1990:

> Large-scale use of radio communications by the LTTE enabled us to listen in to their conversations, identify their voice signatures, radio nets, purpose and general locations and areas of activity. That gave us a fairly good assessment of the militants' strength, areas of operations, types of activity, leaders in terms of who-is-who and who-does-what.

Radio monitoring often enabled the IPKF to follow the movements of key LTTE leaders, such as Velupillai Prabhakaran and Gopalaswami Mahendrarajah (alias Ajit Mahattaya), and to locate their positions with some precision although the IPKF did find that much of its Soviet-supplied DF equipment of the Indian army was inadequate.

On at least two occasions, this communications intelligence was used in an attempt to capture Prabhakaran. As Lt. Gen. Depinder Singh has recounted:

> On one occasion an intercept indicated that Prabhakaran was located in Mulai, a village on the West coast of the Jaffna Peninsula. A raid was mounted by landing Para Commandos

> from the sea. They made rapid progress till they were fired at.... The whole patrol got involved in the desultory firing, giving Prabhakaran ... a chance to escape.

On 11-12 October 1987, when the IPKF mounted a Para Commandos raid to capture Prabhakaran at his residence in central Jaffna, the LTTE had monitored IPKF radio transmissions concerning the operation and laid an ambush for the Indian force; Prabhakaran left the scene two hours before the Indians landed! It was a close call, but in vain.

Lt. Gen. Depinder Singh has recounted how on 12 October, when IPKF Para Commandos mounted the raid on the LTTE's command centre that initiated the battle for Jaffna, monitoring of LTTE communications nets revealed that "from a radio intercept Prabhakaran informed all LTTE stations that the headquarters was under attack and that he may not escape."

LTTE observation posts generally reported the movements of IPKF units over the LTTE communications nets, the monitoring of which provided the IPKF headquarters with useful confirmatory intelligence concerning the particular whereabouts of its own units. As Lt. Gen. Depinder Singh had stated: "The exact location of an IPKF patrol could be discovered by monitoring LTTE communication networks.... It was possible to keep track II; of progress of our patrols by listening to LTTE radio frequencies"!

The LTTE was aware that its radio transmissions were vulnerable to interception and exploitation by the IPKF and Sri Lankan security forces, and it adopted some fairly sophisticated communications security (COMSEC) practices—including frequency hopping transmissions, and the use of codes and ciphers. As Lt. Gen. Sardeshpande has reported:

> The LTTE was also fast to learn, innovative in hardening transmissions and adept at misleading us. Their codes, frequency

> hopping, and methods of transmission became more and more sophisticated. In later months their ground communications and courier system became so efficient that they totally stopped VHF communications in Jaffna Peninsula (and also the Trincomalee Sector). It was indeed hard to break these simple systems....
>
> The (LTTE) had enviable expertise in flexible innovative, reliable and effective communication systems, including codes and ciphers, rarely matched by any other insurgent group the world over.

The LTTE monitored Indian and Sri Lankan military, police and security agency communications. For example, the LTTE maintained a station near Vedaranayam on the south-eastern tip of India, which monitored Tamil Nadu Police messages, which information was used by the LTTE to prepare, for example, an ambush for an Indian paratroop commando attach on the LTTE Jaffna Command Centre on 11-12 October 1987. According to one account: "The LTTE was in fact waiting for the Indians to land—the Tigers had been intercepting the IPKF communications carelessly transmitted to AN PRC-25 VHF sets including the operational details of attacking the LTTE HQ [Command Centre]." (The AN/PRC-25 system used by the IPKF was an unsecure, manpack VHF/FM voice transceiver, designed in the 1950s and produced in the 1960s, which covered the 30-75.95 MHz frequency band, with a maximum transmission range of about five miles.)

With the Tamils in the forefront of the Silicon Valley California e-society, the LTTE recently deployed its scouts in the USA to recruit the best personnel in information technology. The only hitch is the US Government declaring the LTTE as a terrorist organization. But the Sinhala community despite the "marks standardization" measures have been unable to span a similarly high IQ/EQ diaspora. As time passes, and warfare becomes more hi-tech, the Sri Lankan Sinhala army and government will find the battle with LTTE more and more unequal unless some other event makes the battle parameters change [e.g. the Israeli help that had arrived on 5 May 2000 on a plea from President Chandrika currently Indian Navy is providing logistic and Intelligence backing]. But there will be no peace with Prabhakaran because he cannot now settle for anything less than independent Eelam. That is one "tiger" that Prabhakaran dare not dismount! In a press conference a few years ago, Prabhakaran had stated that if he deviated from the Eelam goal, anyone of the LTTE cadre is entitled to shoot him dead. He was making a virtue out of a contingent inevitability.

The Implications of Rajiv Gandhi's Assassination

Having alienated the Indians by providing weapons to the LTTE when it was battling against the IPKF (which, incidentally, had come to Sri Lanka at the request of the Sri Lanka Government and in compliance of treaty obligations under the Indo-Sri Lanka Accord of 1987), the Sinhala community today has painted itself into a corner.

On the other hand, but for Rajiv Gandhi's assassination, Eelam in its real or surrogate from or even an acceptable alternative federal set-up would have been a reality by now. If the Sinhala elite does not come out now to join with the Tamils of the island in a federal or quasi-federal constitutional set-up, the stalemate in Sri Lanka will continue causing further loss of life, grief and pain to all. Then, Eelam will be the only option finally.

But how long will we have to wait? One thing is clear: that Prabhakaran must be brought to book for Rajiv Gandhi's assassination. Even if the Congress Party is callously unconcerned about extraditing Prabhakarn, this is nevertheless the bottom line demand of patriotic Indians. It is revealing that in an interview to a magazine published from New Delhi, the Sri Lankan President

Rajapakse said: "India did not raise this issue with me. The government in New Delhi never asked me to extradite Prabhakaran!" [*Business Economics,* 16-30 November 2006, p. 21.] However, nemisis seems to be catching up with Prabhakaran is becoming increasingly paranoid about capture and the news is that internal conflicts in the LTTE are growing. Since 1993, beginning with the death of Kittu, news began surfacing of internal trouble within the LTTE. The number two person in the LTTE hierarchy, the redoubtable Gopalaswami Mahendrarajah, *alias* Mahatiya was disgraced and later executed on Prabhakaran's order. The head of the outfit's political wing, Yogaratnam, *alias* Yogi was also in trouble. Both were front-ranking cadres who had led their organization in the difficult days of the Indian intervention. They were accused of being RAW agents, and plotting the deaths of the "Tiger" leadership. Then Paris-based Thilagar was recalled and charged with defalcation of funds. The biggest fissure recently came with the walking out of "Karuna," the smart commander of the forces in the East. Despite his best efforts, Prabhakaran has not been able to assassinate Karuna.

Sooner or later, Prabhakaran will be betrayed from inside, especially since the organization cannot grow without getting penetrated. Democratic organizations can survive penetration since the power in such an organization is diffused, and hence cannot be seized. But autocratic terrorist organizations which legitimise violence are destructed the same way—internally.

If it had not been for Prabhakaran's sick compulsion to photograph and chronicle suicide bombing and other terrorist events, Rajiv Gandhi's assassination may have never been unravelled as it has been and the LTTE identified as the assassins. In the dry run for rehearsing the assassination, a Madras-based video film operator was used, but in Rajiv Gandhi's killing, a still photographer, Haribabu, did the needful zealously and hence died in the process. It is possible he was not aware of what was to happen. His last shot was of the explosion itself. One of the pictures showed what later investigation established: the "belt bomb" girl, Dhanu, and Sivarasan posing beside two others who died in the blast.

But it was also Prabhakaran himself who unwittingly provided the first clue as to who Dhanu really was. On 11 June 1991, Prabhakaran emerged out of the shadows to address a public meeting in Jaffna. In that meeting, he made no mention of the assassination of Rajiv Gandhi or even expressed a lip-service regret. But he honoured with the highest award of his organization, A. Rajaratnam, a long-forgotten poet who had died in penury in 1979 in India. I was still a Minister when Prabhakaran made that speech. The speech made IB curious which got on the job to find out. A Tamil refugee source gave us the clue: Rajaratnam's only claim to fame was his Tamil Black Tigress daughter Gayatri, also known as Dhanu. An old LTTE magazine retrieved by us had her photo, and it matched with Dhanu. Obviously, Prabhakaran did not have the nerve to publicly honour Dhanu for killing Rajiv Gandhi. So he honoured her father. The identification clinched, *prima facie* the LTTE's role in the assassination.

In 1990, LTTE assassins, led by the same Sivarasan, had managed to gun down the well-guarded EPRLF leader K. Padmanabha, and escape after a 350 km-drive through the night to Pillayar Thidal on the Thanjavur coast. In contrast, the group of assassins of Rajiv Gandhi wandered in different safe houses until their final entrapment and suicide on 19 August 1991 at a safe house in Konanakunte, near Bangalore. It is possible that LTTE had avoided the Vedaranyam route for escape because the DMK was no more in power in the state. On the other hand, enormous self-confidence, verging on bravado, had been the characteristic of the top LTTE operatives, and the ease with which they had operated in Tamil Nadu prior to Rajiv Gandhi's assassination could have contributed to this complacency. But most of all, if the government on Indian soil is not sympathetic, the LTTE is out of its depths. That was the difference in the two assassinations—Padmanabha's and Rajiv Gandhi's.

The SIT's case against the LTTE was also strengthened by five letters, seized in the wake of the investigation. Three were written by the core squad to LTTE intelligence chief Pottu Amman and the women's wing chief Akila (now dead in battle). Dhanu and her stand-by Subha reiterated their loyalty to the outfit and gleefully described their 7 May penetration of V.P. Singh's election meeting. These letters were to have gone across to Jaffna from Vedaranyam, but the courier returned to Madras, after having buried them for safekeeping, when the boat to take them across to Jaffna failed to turn up. More damning of the LTTE was a letter from the LTTE "coordinator" in India, "Gundu" Santhan, to LTTE chief V. Prabhakaran in September 1991. This letter was on the person of Irumborai of DK an "Indian" stooge organization of the LTTE—when while trying to cross to Jaffna he was arrested on 30 October 1991, at Rameshwaram. Santhan described the problems faced by the group with the SIT hot on their heels, and the suicide of the core group. An accompanying note to Irumborai advised him *to tell Prabhakaran to disclaim all foreknowledge of the assassination plot.*

With Dhanu identified, some arrests followed. The process of nabbing the culprits was under way. By 20 May 1992, the SIT filed the chargesheet, and the trial began on 5 May 1993. On 28 January 1998, the trial court sentenced all 26 to hang for the assassination. The SIT held firmly to the stand that all evidence pointed to LTTE and LTTE alone as the agency that carried out the assassination of Rajiv Gandhi.

On behalf of the convicted persons, the LTTE organized through its *de facto* front organizations in India an appeal against the trial court verdict.

On 12 May 1999, the Supreme Court upheld the guilty verdict of the trial court; but since the apex court held that the provisions of the Terrorist and Disruptive Activities Act (TADA) did not apply in this crime, only four of the 26 persons were declared deserving of the death penalty under the Indian Penal Code.

The two main accused, LTTE supremo V. Prabhakaran and his deputy Pottu Amman, were declared "Proclaimed Offenders" for failing to surrender to court, and their trial was held in abeyance till they are caught and brought to court to face the charges of murder of Rajiv Gandhi.

The LTTE moved the Supreme Court to review their judgement. On 5 October 1999, the Supreme Court rejected the plea of the review as devoid of any merit. The hanging of the four convicted persons was fixed for 5 November 1999. It has not yet been carried out. Why?

Incredibly, the answer is: because of a letter written by Ms Sonia Gandhi, the widow, to the President of India with a copy to the Tamil Nadu Governor, seeking clemency for the killers! There is no letter or appeal from the convicted killers to Ms Gandhi seeking mercy. It was a *suo-moto* appeal by Mrs Gandhi. The matter is still pending as the letter of the Home Minister to me appended here shows.

The Congress Party, in the meantime, has also gone strangely silent on the issue of Prabhakaran's extradition, after Ms Sonia Gandhi for inexplicable reasons asked for clemency for those sent to the gallows to be hanged under the Supreme Court's verdict. Clemency is for those who commit murder in a momentary fit of passion, and those who otherwise are fit members of society. They must plead for mercy. The Supreme Court in its judgement recorded the admission of the LTTE counsel of those in death row, that they cold bloodedly wanted Rajiv Gandhi dead to avenge India's national policy decision to despatch IPKF (for which the LTTE held Rajiv Gandhi personally liable), and more importantly to prevent him from becoming Prime Minister again. There is no passion here, no

L. K. ADVANI
HOME MINISTER

D.O. No. I-11034/36/2000-ISDI(A)

Dear Dr. Swamy Ji,

19 SEP 2000

Kindly refer to your letter dated 11th April, 2000 regarding execution of death sentence on the four LTTE conspirators in the Rajiv Gandhi assassination case and imposition of ban on LTTE.

2. The prisoners Ms. S. Nalini and S/Shri Suthenthiraraja @ Santhan, Sriharan @ Murugan and Pararivalan@ Arivu convicted and sentenced to death in the Rajiv Gandhi assassination case, have submitted Petitions to the President of India for consideration under article 72 of the Constitution of India. These petitions are under consideration.

3. There is no such ruling that the death sentence of a prisoner shall automatically stand commuted to life imprisonment if the State fails to execute the sentence within one year.

4. The Central Government declared the LTTE as an unlawful association on 14.5.2000.

With regards,

Yours sincerely,

L. K. Advani

(L.K. Advani)

Dr. Subramanian Swamy,
President, Janata Party,
A-77, Nizamuddin (East),
New Delhi-110013.

Ministry of Home Affairs, North Block New Delhi -110001 INDIA
"Please visit our website at http://mha. nic.in"

temporary insanity. It was a premeditated act to destroy a national investment, which all experienced patriotic political leaders in a democratic society are. Rajiv Gandhi did not show mercy for his mother's killer, Satwant Singh, nor Jawaharlal Nehru showed for Nathuram Godse who killed Mahatma Gandhi.

The Unanswered Questions in Rajiv Gandhi's Assassination

The question who or which organization carried out the assassination was thus decisively answered by the SIT led by CBI Director Kartikeyan, and upheld by the Supreme Court. But other questions remain unanswered and some have event not been asked.

The evidence, so far produced in regard to Rajiv Gandhi's assassination, should make the nation look beyond the usual retribution. Although the nation has accepted the Supreme Court's final verdict that it was the LTTE-led by Prabhakaran which had ordered, planned and executed the conspiracy to assassinate Rajiv Gandhi to avenge the alleged atrocities of the IPKF, there are nevertheless unanswered questions. While *these have no bearing on the final view of the Supreme Court and no relevance to the CBI/SIT prosecution case that has been upheld by two courts,* queries nevertheless have to be asked in the interest of truth and for safeguarding the nation from the enemies within, and from the human and financial network they operate in. Residual questions need to be answered for achieving a more secure India. In particular, it is imperative in the national interest to expose those who wittingly and knowingly *facilitated* the LTTE to carry out its dirty dastardly deed of killing Rajiv Gandhi and who thereafter (even if vainly) tried to pin the murder charge on others to save the LTTE. Since the LTTE killed Rajiv Gandhi, they cannot be allowed to get away with it. We can learn a lesson here from the Americans who, to avenge the murder of their ordinary citizens on board the *Pan Am Jet* (that had exploded mid-air over Lockable, i.e. Scotland), went to such lengths to search for the culprits that the culprits' safe haven, Libya, had to finally meekly hand them over, or face ruin. A people justifiably can be proud of such a state.

In any case, whether the LTTE was facilitated in the assassination of Rajiv Gandhi by Indians or even that LTTE agreed to a "Supari," i.e. a contract killing for some Indians or foreigners, in either case it impinges on the feasibility of a solution to the Sri Lanka crisis. Indeed empowering the LTTE or even legitimizing the LTTE as a party to a settlement is loaded with serious national security implications.

A legitimized or empowered LTTE can be relied on to function as a cat's paw for nefarious forces within India who may want to change the direction of Indian politics by resorting to contract killing. Hence, we need to punish all those involved in the assassination of Rajiv Gandhi.

At the very least, Prabhakaran and Pottu Amman have to be brought to trial. Extradition was to be the top-most task for the Multi-Disciplinary Monitoring Agency (MDMA) constituted in 1998 but, despite their being nearly eight years to date on the job, they have not got anywhere; or perhaps they have done nothing because there are and have been pro-LTTE ministers and politicians in power in Delhi since 1998. Hence, the MDMA may have *not* got the necessary political clearances. Therefore, unless there is a national clamour, the kingpin of Rajiv Gandhi's assassination will not be apprehended because the MDMA, tasked by an insincere government, would under the ruling coalition's pressure remain paralysed on this issue.

What is significant is that the assassination of Rajiv Gandhi was not a hit-and-run affair, but had culminated in a sequence of planned and unplanned events. The first was *his character assassination in the IPKF atrocities*—as if the despatch of the army to Sri Lanka was his *personal* decision and that he was *personally* responsible for all the atrocities. The liberals and bleeding hearts, many of them financed by the LTTE, raised a cacophony about it. The IPKF decision was a natural corollary of the united Tamil demand (including the LTTE) that "Mother" India must stand guarantee for any accord of Tamils with Sri Lanka Government. The Sinhalas did not want it, but India rammed it down their throats by *Operation Pumalai* and international acquiescence in the same. Parliament had fully endorsed the sending of the IPKF, making it a national policy. And yet after the LTTE had welched on its commitment and joined hands with the same Sinhalas (against whose "Aryan arrogance" and insensitivity, the IPKF had been despatched), it was sadly Rajiv Gandhi who was left holding the bag.

If anyone betrayed the Tamils at that juncture, it was Prabhakaran who shook hands with that notorious Tamil–and India-hater, President Premadasa, to humiliate and send back the IPKF. Prabhakaran had collaborators in this dastardly act in India, of course, who sang a wild chorus of the Indian Army's brutalities. These persons are thus the facilitators of the first stage in the assassination. They or their people have been rewarded with ministerships in the Union Government of today! But this character assassination made it easy for Prabhakaran to find recruits willing to die, and in the process to take Rajiv Gandhi's life with them. Character assassination generally precedes physical assassination because the killer must hate before he can kill. For Godse to kill, the fanatics had by word of mouth propaganda character-assassinated Mahatma Gandhi—that he had sold out to Pakistan, and was forcing the government to hand over India's treasury to that country. Godse then killed like a robot inspired, by this sick propaganda imbibed in him.

The second stage in Rajiv Gandhi's assassination came when Prabhakaran was provoked to act with urgency. Rajiv Gandhi was voted out of office, and the IPKF had been pulled out. The V.P. Singh Government with DMK as partner had converted Tamil Nadu as a sanctuary for the LTTE, as a military hinterland that nursed its injured and produced its battle needs. Chief Minister Karunanidhi refused even to receive and welcome back home troops which had gone to obey Parliament's will. This ought to have warmed the cockles of the LTTE "heart." Rivals like the EPRLF were decimated in broad day-light in Chennai. (In a gory cine style killing, the AK-47 toting assassins sprayed bullets, whereafter the visiting killers were even given a send off.) Vaiko even proved that a passport for travel was not necessary to go and pay obeiscence to Prabhakaran. Nedumaran had not wanted to be left behind, but alas his boat sprung a leak and it had sunk. Tamil Nadu police had to rescue a very wet LTTE commissar. There was even a possibility that the LTTE could draw on Mother India's Tamil population for recruits to a force which the LTTE set up calling it a Tamil Nadu Retrieval Army (*sic*).

When it looked as if everything was set for the LTTE, the V.P. Singh Government began to wobble and totter over the Mandal and masjid issues. It seems then President Premadasa had become quite panic-stricken at the thought that an election could bring back the "hated" Rajiv Gandhi as Prime Minister. He probably had no idea then that there could be another government [of Chandrashekhar] installed before that. But in August 1990 (12-8-90 and 19-8-90 issues) the *Sunday* made Rajiv Gandhi go on record on what was then a dead issue, on the hypothetical question whether if he returned as PM, would he re-despatch the IPKF (obviously to disarm the LTTE again), and whether he defended his earlier decision to sign the Indo-Sri Lanka accord. Rajiv Gandhi walked into that landmine and said a firm yes to both questions. Alarm bells rang in north and south Sri Lanka, and the two affected persons, Prabhakaran and Premadasa, must have been galvanized, and may be the two had even consulted each other—after all they were formal allies till June 1990 and became open enemies only after Rajiv Gandhi's assassination.

The Supreme Court held [*State vs. Nalini,* (1999) 5 SCC 385] that "the conspiracy was activated with the publication of an interview in the *Sunday* Magazine," then edited by Vir Sanghvi. It was published in the August 21-28 issue of the magazine. It is now known that Prabhakaran sent his first team of "sleepers" in the first week of September 1990, to set up the network for carrying out the assassination. Prabhakaran had perhaps learnt from past attempt(s) that without access and being physical proximity to Rajiv Gandhi it would not be possible to succeed in the assassination attempt. The IB has, in its records, an uncorroborated wireless intercept, that the LTTE had planned to assassinate Rajiv Gandhi on 18 June 1988 when he came to Chennai as Prime Minister by "welcoming" him with, what the intercept called, a "garland of bullets," but it found that the assassins could not get near him. I presume that during this unholy *inter-regnum,* Prabhakaran must have been enthused by a fiction thriller novel in which a human bomb *femme fatale* kills her target by climbing the stage at a public function to offer him a bouquet of flowers, thereby disarming even the security detail. In other words, the human bomb idea was not original to the LTTE.

The third stage of the LTTE's planning came when the general mid-term election to Parliament looked inevitable in mid-February 1991. Had the Chandrashekhar Government (of which I was the senior-most Minister) not fallen, Rajiv Gandhi would have been alive today, because we had just about commenced smashing the LTTE's deep-rooted network in Tamil Nadu, after dismissing the DMK Government. In a year's time, there would have been no LTTE anywhere in Tamil Nadu. As it was, with DMK on the run, the LTTE had managed to retain a modicum of its base by developing its Congress Party commercial contacts through Shanmugham, P.V. Rajendran, and J. Paramanand. With President's Rule in the state, Congressmen were naturally less suspect. The LTTE also developed close relations through as yet uninvestigated commercial contact with Ms Jayalalitha's close associate Sasikala's husband, Natarajan. I leave the reader with a puzzle as to why just after the assassination, some members of the AIADMK filed for anticipatory bail in the Madras High Court in anticipation of possible arrest in the assassination case (*Statesman*'s Sam Rajappa was the only one with the nerve to file this story). Thus the third stage of positioning the killer squad led by Sivarasan in various parts of Tamil Nadu was facilitated by the sea coast-based contraband maestro and local Congress leader Shanmugham and his associates. It is a sad commentary on the state of affairs in the country, on how much money can buy in India, something the young terrorist Athirai had contemptuously told SIT chief Kartikeyan during her interrogation.

The fourth stage of the assassination planning came in ensuring that Rajiv Gandhi came to Tamil Nadu again, and that in the meeting that he would address, the killer squad including Dhanu got the necessary access to him. This was the most crucial stage of facilitation. It is now well established that Rajiv Gandhi had been cajoled into coming back to Tamil Nadu to campaign (even though the leaders in responsible positions at the ground level, such as Tamil Nadu Congress President Vazhapadi Ramamurthy, the alliance partner Ms Jayalalitha, the Sriperumbudur Congress candidate Chandrashekar, Congress leader G.K. Moopanar not to mention the Governor and the security personnel, were quite against the need for his trip). It was not that they knew something would go wrong, but that it was not worth Rajiv Gandhi's while. Furthermore, once he had taken the decision and come had the Congress local organizers not interfered with security arrangements, Rajiv Gandhi would have been safe even at the level of security provided for him. [Intelligence officers have anonimously spoken to the media as the extract of a news item appended here shows.]

The Justice J.S. Verma Commission has categorically stated that it was access control that had failed, and not security infrastructure *per se*. The demolished access control was decisive for the success

AICC collusion with LTTE not explored: Intelligence officer

By Janak Singh

NEW DELHI: Senior Intelligence Officials view Congress attempts to pin the blame for the assassination of Rajiv Gandhi on Dravida Munnetra Khazhagam (DMK) as a red herring to divert attention from All India Congress Committee's (AICC) role in the tragedy.

"The phone records of Madras Raj Bhavan, AICC and 10, Janpath, on the day of the assassination (21 May 1991) will show that it was on the insistence of Congress VIPs that Rajiv Gandhi went to Sriperumbudur," said a former adviser to the Tamil Nadu Governor in 1991. He added that the Tamil Nadu administration had clearly warned Rajiv Gandhi "against going to Sriperumbudur."

A Senior intelligence officer disclosed: "Top members of AICC actually wanted Rajiv Gandhi to spend the night in Sriperumbudur at the home of a rich Congressman. Then it was pointed out that Rajiv Gandhi's proposed bedroom was immediately above a godown where explosive could have been stored.

Only then did the AICC bigwigs agree that Rajiv Gandhi should return to Madras after making the speech at Sriperumbudur."

Top intelligence officials claimed that the then Tamil Nadu administration as well as the Intelligence Bureau sent several warnings to 10, Janpath, advising against the visit. "Senior Congress leaders including some who are today loudest in shedding crocodile tears, refused to listen and insisted that Rajiv Gandhi should go to that unsafe place," a senior IB official said. When asked to give names, he mentioned Margaret Alva as one of those in favour of Rajiv Gandhi going to Sriperumbudur.

"For reasons of its own the Jain Commission has not investigated the link between the LTTE and top members of Congress in Tamil Nadu," a senior Tamil Nadu official said. "For example, LTTE sympathisers were given passes and other assistance by the family of the then AICC general secretary Maragatham Chandrashekhar," he alleged, pointing out that Chandrashekhar's daughter is even today a prominent Congress leader in Tamil Nadu. "This lady accompanied several dangerous pro-LTTE elements into the inner cordon. Why didn't the Jain Commission investigate her thoroughly, the Tamil Nadu Officials asked...

The Times of India, 18 November 1997.
Reproduced in *Buried Facts,* Dravida Munnetra
Kazgham, Chennai, August 1998.

ANNEXURE XXX

R. M. CRASH SECRET

TO : DC HQRS, MADRAS.

Ss.P., CH.A. (E) CH.A. (W), TAN(E), PTT, SLM & DPI DCP, AIRPORT SECURITY, MADRAS.

INFN : COP, MDS

D.Is.G., CH.A. TRI, MDU & VLR RANGES
DETT. INSPRS., SB CID, CH.A.(E), CH.A.(W), TAN(E), PTT., SLM & DPI
IG, FOREST CELL, CID & IG, HOME GUARDS, MADRAS
IG, ARMED POLICE, CAMP AT TRICHY

FROM : DIG CID (I) MADRAS

SCA.I.No.4623-I/T DT. 19-5-91

PLEASE REFER THIS BRANCH R.M. SCA.I.No. 4623/T DATED 18-5-91 REGARDING VISIT OF THIRU RAJIV GANDHI, FORMER PRIME MINISTER OF INDIA TO TAMIL NADU ON 21-5-91 AND 22-5-91.

FOLLOWING IS THE DETAILED TOUR PROGRAMME OF VIP :

21-5-91	1815 hrs	DEP.	VISAKHAPATTINAM BY SPECIAL AIRCRAFT.
	1935 hrs	ARR.	MEENAMBAKKAM AIRPORT
	2000 hrs	DEP.	MEENAMBAKKAM AIRPORT BY ROAD
	2100 hrs	ARR.	SRIPERUMBUDUR. ADDRESSES PUBLIC MEETING. NIGHT HALT.
22-5-91	0700 hrs	DEP.	SRIPERUMBUDUR BY HELICOPTER
	0740 hrs	ARR.	PONDICHERRY
	0840 hrs	DEP.	PONDICHERRY BY HELICOPTER.
	0920 hrs	ARR.	MAYILADUTHURAI. ADDRESSES PUBLIC MEETING.
	1020 hrs	DEP.	MAYILADUTHURAI BY HELICOPTER
	1115 hrs	ARR.	SIVAGANGAI. ADDRESSES PUBLIC MEETING.
	1255 hrs	DEP.	SIVAGANGAI BY HELICOPTER
	1455 hrs	ARR.	SALEM. ADDRESSES PUBLIC MEETING
	1515 hrs	DEP.	SALEM BY HELICOPTER
	1555 hrs	ARR.	KRISHNAGIRI. ADDRESSES PUBLIC MEETING.
	1700 hrs	DEP.	KRISHNAGIRI BY HELICOPTER
	1730 hrs	ARR.	BANGALORE
	1800 hrs	DEP.	BANGALORE FOR DELHI BY AIR.

PLEASE MAKE NECESSARY SECURITY ARRANGEMENTS AS PER THE INSTRUCTION ISSUED IN THIS BRANCH R.M. CITED ABOVE.

FAILURE OF PUBLIC ADDRESS SYSTEM IN A PUBLIC MEETING ADDRESSED BY A VVIP IN ONE PLACE LED CONFUSION AND LAW AND ORDER PROBLEM. THEREFORE THE PUBLIC ADDRESS SYSTEM SHOULD BE CHECKED FOR ITS EFFECTIVENESS IN CONSULTATION WITH LOCAL PARTY LEADERS.

LIGHTING ARRANGEMENTS MAY ALSO BE GOT MADE IN CONSULTATION WITH LOCAL PARTY LEADERS TO AVOID CONFUSION AND MISCHIEF IN CASE OF THE PUBLIC MEETING GETS DELAYED DUE TO ANY POSSIBLE DELAY IN THE ARRIVAL OF THE VIP.

IT MAY BE REMEMBERED THAT THERE WAS AN ATTEMPT SUSPECTED TO BE BY SIKH EXTREMISTS ON THE LIFE OF FORMER UNION MINISTER THIRU JAGDISH TYTLER AT NEW DELHI ON 17-5-91 WHILE HE WAS ADDRESSING A PUBLIC MEETING IN WHICH FORMER UNION MINISTER NARROWLY ESCAPED WHILE TWO OTHERS SUCCUMBED TO BULLET INJURIES. THEREFORE IT IS DESIRABLE IN THE INTEREST OF SECURITY TO ENFORCE A STERILE AREA OF 45 FEET RADIUS AROUND THE ROSTRUM. IT MAY BE GOT DONE IN LIAISON WITH THE LOCAL PARTY LEADERS AND THE FOLLOWING PRECAUTIONS MAY BE TAKEN DURING THE VISITS OF THIRU RAJIV GANDHI :—

(i) STRICT ACCESS CONTROL IN THE VICINITY OF THE PROTECTED PERSON;

(ii) PROPER POSITIONING OF AN ALERT AND WELL TRAINED RING ROUND TEAM NEAR HIM;

(iii) POSITIONING OF WELL TRAINED STRIKING RESERVES WITH ADEQUATE FIRE POWER IN VEHICLE CLOSE TO HIM TO OPERATE AS AN ANTI-TERRORIST SQUAD; AND

(iv) ADEQUATE ANTI-SABOTAGE PRECAUTIONS DURING ALL HIS PROGRAMMES.

(P. C. MUTHUSAMY)
Sd/-
for DIG CID (I) MDS

Copy to the Inspectors VIP Section and Administration.
Copy to the Dy. Supdt. of Police, SB CID, Security, Madras.
DG/ADG/IG/(L&O)/IG (I)/DIG (I)/SSB/SP/(S) I/SP (S) II/SP 'Q' :
Sir,

For favour of perusal after issue.

(True copy)

ATTESTED

P. SUBBARAYAN
MANAGER S. B.C.I.D.
(SECURITY) MADRAS.

Dr Subramanian Swamy Ph.D. (Harvard)
President, Janata Party (1989 -)
Minister for Commerce, Law & Justice (1990-91)
Chairman (with Cabinet rank)
Commission on Labour Standards (1994-96)
Professor of Economics IIT Delhi (1969-91) &
Faculty of Economics, Harvard (1963-9, 1985-6, 2000-2)

JANATA PARTY

A-77, Nizamuddin (East) New Delhi - 110 013
Phone 4353805 Fax 4357386
Mobile : 9810194279
Website : www.janata.org
E-mail swamy@post.harvard.edu

February 16, 2004

Mr. L.K. Advani
Deputy Prime Minister
Ministry of Home Affairs
New Delhi--110011

Dear Advanji,

My usually reliable sources inform me that Congress President Ms. Sonia Gandhi has sent an emissary to Sri Lanka to meet the LTTE leaders including the supremo V.Prabhakaran, who is a proclaimed offender in the Rajiv Gandhi assassination case. The Interpol has also issued a world wide Red Corner Notice for apprehending him. The emissary is former Minister of State for External Affairs, Eduardo Falerio. He travelled from Delhi to Trivandrum and then to Colombo. I believe that Kerala Congress president Murlidharan may have arranged his air ticket and stay in Trivandrum. The Chief Minister appears to be in the know too.

Last evening Mr.Falerio arrived in Jaffna, and is staying as a guest of the Vice Chancellor of Jaffna University. Jaffna based LTTE Commissar, one Padmanathan is to accompany Mr. Falerio to Killonochi for a possible meeting with Prabhakaran. The agenda for the meeting was decided in London when Falerio was possibly there, and communicated by Anton Balasingham to Prabhakaran's headquarters. I am informed that the agenda is about coming elections and what to do about the Tamil Nadu Chief Minister Ms.Jayalalitha.

At the very least Mr.Falerio should on his return be interrogated.
He has no reason to be in Jaffna except for mischief. You may also consider reviewing the security cover for Ms.Jayalalitha, and in particular determine if there are any LTTE moles at her residence.

During my many meetings with you during the last five years I have repeatedly protested to you about the soft approach of your government on LTTE terrorism. Time has now to deal with the LTTE menace decisively.

Yours Sincerely,

(SUBRAMANIAN SWAMY)

of the assassination attempt. [See appended instructions of the police.] Let me reiterate that the disruption by local Congress leaders of the security arrangements may have not been *mala fide* or had anything to do with the assassination plot. Only a proper inquiry in the future can tell for certain, but the LTTE knew how to penetrate the security arrangements because they had understood Congress culture. For that they got the necessary introductions from amongst the local Congress organizers, and perhaps even the police; but whether or not it was deliberate should have been probed by the government since the Verma Commission had recommended it. Unfortunately, Prime Minister Narasimha Rao's Cabinet rejected the idea. In the same way, the LTTE managed to get Rajiv Gandhi's tour programme well in advance from AICC office-bearers as two of the accused in the trial had claimed. But Congress leaders' connections and contacts with the LTTE continue even today [see appended letter written by me to the Home Minister].

We need to authentically find out how Rajiv Gandhi was cajoled into going to Sriperumbudur, how his tour programme was leaked, and why the security arrangements at Sriperumbudur were wantonly flouted. Was it achieved by LTTE by money or blackmail or something else? In any case, it will not alter an iota of what we already believe to be true, contained in the substance of the court verdicts, holding the LTTE responsible for having committed Rajiv Gandhi's murder. And yet the nation needs to know all dimensions of the above-delineated facilitation that took place. Clearly the facilitation at this stage was done by local Congress organizers. And hence the question needs to be addressed: was the assassination a contract, "Supari" job, by the LTTE? And if so, for whom? Who benefitted monetarily and politically by Rajiv Gandhi's assassination?

The fifth stage set into motion by Pottu Amman, and taken judicial notice of by the Supreme Court, is the LTTE's attempt to deny their involvement in the assassination and to blame the CIA/Mossad for it, For this purpose, the LTTE had mobilized (according to the decoded wireless intercepts of Pottu Amman's conversation with Sivarasan, after the assassination), their friends in "high places" in India. Thereafter, the nation did witness a chorus as *if orchestrated,* from several prominent persons, *all giving credence to the same story:* That the assassination was masterminded by the CIA or Mossad or both (in which by innuendos P.V. Narasimha Rao and Chandraswami had co-operated). And that precisely was what was repeatedly denied by all the governmental investigative and intelligence agencies, besides Cabinet Secretaries, Home Secretaries, and Foreign Secretaries who while in office had deposed so on oath before the Jain Commission. That, incidentally, was what was also denied by two courts, including the apex court—the Supreme Court sitting as a three-judge Bench. Then what was the motive of these highly placed individuals to try and seek the exoneration of the LTTE? Was there some one higher who could bring all these people together to propagate such a lie?

Rajiv Gandhi disliked Arjun Singh and was planning to dump him after the 1991 elections. *Rajiv Gandhi told me so.* Already, when Prime Minister, he had him investigated by Home Minister Buta Singh on reports of corruption in the Churhat Lottery scandal and the Union Carbide gas leak cover up. Rajiv Gandhi had learnt from Giani Zail Singh that it was Arjun Singh who first had mooted that the President of India should take the unprecedented step of sacking Prime Minister Rajiv Gandhi on the Bofors scandal, and anointing him in his place, in return for a second term for Giani as President! There is also as yet uninvestigated information that since Rajiv Gandhi showed no signs of coming to Tamil Nadu, Sivarasan and Dhanu had first tried to assassinate Rajiv Gandhi in Bhopal on 12 May (Rajiv Gandhi was to stop over in Bhopal on a trip from Goa enroute to Delhi). The plot fizzled out because as Tamils the assassins team could not get close to Rajiv Gandhi without illiciting the attracting the special interest of the intelligence agents.

Incidentally, the former Director General of Police in Tamil Nadu, an exceptionally straight-forward officer by name K. Mohan Das, on whom MGR placed full confidence in dealings with the LTTE, and perhaps thus he had continued to be in touch with them even after his retirement, wrote a novel, *The Assassination* (published by Lancer), which appeared in print in 1993, in which a character by name Nero plots to kill the Prime Minister of a country. The script is strikingly similar to Rajiv Gandhi's assassination plot. With some difficulty (because there are many red herrings), I could decipher the names. I met the former DGP before his sudden death, to query him, but he was wholly uncommunicative on the issue. He neither confirmed nor denied my decoding of the characters in his novel, or said why he had to pen a novel at all. But he did concede that the novel was about Rajiv Gandhi's assassination and that he was writing a sequel which was on his computer diskette. What happened to the diskette only his family members can tell. While on such a serious matter we cannot, of course, give credence or importance to dreams, novels, or crystal balls as Justice Jain had done, nevertheless to Mohan Das' credit he did not go out to seek publicity or even offered to depose before the Commission on this issue.

We can now move on from the question as to who or why Rajiv Gandhi was killed (which the Supreme Court has firmly established) to the question as to who had helped the LTTE first in facilitation and then in its disinformation blame game, even if all of it was finally in vain, and ask why it was at all attempted? A close reading of the Apex Court judgement confirms the disinformation campaign launched since Rajiv Gandhi's assassination, which campaign was to deny, or at the very least dilute, the LTTE involvement in the assassination, and to scandalize those *who had dared to challenge this disinformation campaign.*

The Supreme Court had taken judicial notice of this disinformation campaign, noting (para 555 at page 503) that "in the present case, the LTTE tried to conceal the fact that it was behind the murder of Rajiv Gandhi." The Apex Court quotes from a wireless message sent the day after the assassination by the LTTE intelligence Chief (one of the three absconding accused) Pottu Amman to Sivarasan that "*even to* our people in higher places we informed that we have no connection with this" (*ibid.*).

Now, of course, having been convicted for the assassination, the LTTE has gone on another ploy: to express regret, and say forgive us and forget the murder. This tragic-comic stance is typical of the LTTE which thinks that they can commit murder and get away it by denying it or expressing regret.

When the LTTE ideologue, Anton Stanilaus *nee* Balasingham, recently made a public statement that the terrorist organization "regrets" the assassination and "requests" India to put it behind it in a fit of large heartedness or amnesia, he had miscalculated that India would discount the perfidy of the assassination and move on. He was in for a surprise. The nation reacted with guffaws and sneers. So strong was the reaction that even the Prime Minister had to cancel his appointment to meet the visiting Sri Lanka MPs who owed alliegiance to the LTTE. The LTTE should have known better about the Indian sentiment. The Union Home Ministry *Annual Report (2004-05) to Parliament* gave expression to this intrinsic Indian attitude toward the LTTE as follows:

> 3.150 The Liberation Tigers of Tamil Eelam (The LTTE) which was first declared as "an unlawful association" under the Unlawful Activities (Prevention) Act 1967, on 14 May 1992 was further notified as an unlawful association on 1994, 1996, 1998, 2000 and 2002 after complying with the procedure laid down under the Act. The ban has been further extended for a period of two years w.e.f. 14 May 2004.
>
> 3.151 The LTTE continues to be an extremely potent, most lethal and well-organized terrorist force in Sri Lanka and has strong connections in Tamil Nadu and certain pockets of southern India. The organization assiduously cultivates the

> Tamil Chauvinist elements who are inspired by the Tamil Eelam concept of a separate Tamil Nadu i.e., session from India. The LTTE by carrying out several successful suicide-killing missions in Sri Lanka and one in India has emerged as one of the deadliest terrorist organization in the world, which has sympathizers, supporters and agents on the Indian soil.
>
> 3.152 Notwithstanding the current peace process, the LTTE is yet to give up violence as a means to achieve its goal of establishing a separate homeland for Tamils. *Further, it is well known that the LTTE Intelligence Wing maintains exhaustive data on personalities who are opposed to the outfit's ideology for engineering their assassination, if considered necessary.* The LTTE continues to use the State of Tamil Nadu as a base of carrying out smuggling of essential items like petrol, diesel besides drugs to Sri Lanka. The LTTE's insistence on recognition of sea Tigers as a separate unit by the Sri Lankan Government poses yet another threat to Indian security. [*Source:* Annual Report to Parliament (2004-05); Ministry of Home Affairs, New Delhi.]

Since the Supreme Court has in definitive terms laid down as to who had organized the assassination of Rajiv Gandhi, and that the LTTE conspirators had pleaded guilty before the highest court in the land to the charge, the nation must now move on to discover the identity of those in the "higher places" in India on whom the LTTE had depended all these years for the vicious and sinister disinformation campaign to try and get them off the hook on the charge of murder. These persons may not been active conspirators in the murder of Rajiv Gandhi, *but they certainly are at least guilty of impeding the investigation and attempting to confound the evidence.* They also are guilty of betraying the country since Rajiv Gandhi's assassination is a challenge to our sovereignty and an insult to our national self-respect.

The list of facilitators is quite long. There must be many more behind them. All of them are, in the eyes of law, at least *accessories after the fact.*

The story thus does not end here even if we have to pause now for some time because in confronting the LTTE, the government in office today is constrained by its own coalition composition (since it contains pro-LTTE parties) and the consequent compulsions that arise. Regrettably, most politicians are frightened, and more regrettably still, quite a few are up for sale. But the nation cannot afford to forget the assassination of Rajiv Gandhi, or even to forgive the people responsible for it. For, it was not only Rajiv Gandhi who was bodily destroyed in Sriperumbudur along with 15 other unsuspecting persons, mostly police persons on duty; with them a significant part of India's sovereignty and national self-respect was destructed. Hence, India cannot participate in implementing any options in which the LTTE has a place. Any alternative solution has to rule out as unfeasible the LTTE as a part of that solution. *The LTTE is part of the problem, and has to be dealt with, with that in focus.*

Tamils must in any solution have an area or areas that they can sub-administer with well-defined devolution of powers. The author recommends that the Indian-type Constitution, with the Centre's hegemony and several states of the Sri Lanka Union, is the best arrangement. India must exercise its substantial influence to see that the Sri Lanka Parliament agrees to this.

Indian national interest cannot afford that its Prime Minister today waffle on the issue. The central question is, whether India, in particular India *alone,* should intervene in Sri Lanka (preferably on Sri Lanka's invitation) and if so, how, when, and at what price?

In 1987, following the failure of the 1986 Thimpu (Bhutan) peace conference of Sri Lankan Tamil leaders and the government of the island at the Sri Lankan Tamil minority's insistence as a precondition for a peace agreement, India had intervened, which insistence had been conveyed by *all* Tamil groups of Sri

Lanka to the then Prime Minister Rajiv Gandhi. The LTTE was a party to that insistence then, but as terrorist organizations are prone to do, the LTTE soon after IPKF intervention welshed on its commitment—as it realized that India was not going to carve out Eelam and hand it over to the LTTE. Soon thereafter the LTTE struck a profitable but a perfidious and clandestine deal with Premadasa (the then Sri Lankan President). The deal, now revealed by a Commission of Inquiry in Colombo, was for the Sri Lankan Government to supply weapons and provide logistic support to the LTTE. In turn, the LTTE would fight the IPKF. It was the most dastardly betrayal of India, a country once described by the LTTE supremo Prabhakaran as the "mother country," thus proving the old adage: "Words are cheap."

The message from the decade of the 1980s for India is thus crystal clear: we are damned if we do, and damned if we don't. More importantly, the Sri Lankan problem will not go away even if we look the other way much as an ostrich would do. It is bound to get worse alternatively due to the Sinhala current mindset ("no sharing of power in devolution with Tamils") and LTTE's terrorism (kill and deal, deal and kill). Thus if we do not intervene, then sooner or later we will suffer the consequences of the conflict which will be worse than if we had intervened. The question that remains is as to the extent and the limit of that intervention.

Chapter Three

India's Options:
The Scope and Limits of Intervention

We have to move forward now to assess India's options to end Sri Lanka's crisis. At the outset India must identify as qualified to be a part of the solution, only those who have well established credentials of being anti-terrorists in general and opposed to LTTE in particular, since only they would be acceptable to the Sinhala people as well.

Since the LTTE has brutalized the Sinhalas, a pro-LTTE facilitation team from India will not be welcome in Colombo. Therein lies the dilemma for the Indian Prime Minister, since his government's majority at the margin depends on pro-LTTE parties such as the DMK and PMK, while it is the imperative of national security that LTTE be kept out and dealt with as a terrorist outfit.

India's policy towards this internationally proclaimed terrorist organization, the Liberation Tigers of Tamil Eelam (LTTE), now requires to be sharply defined before it is too late. Now is the moment of truth for clarity and transparency. Otherwise, one more neighbour, Sri Lanka, after Pakistan, Bangladesh, and Nepal could become a breeding ground for anti-Indian terrorists. Hence, India has no option but to intervene at some point in the near future. And only India can do so effectively.

My queries have led me to believe with confidence that there is no other power in the world that feels compelled to intervene in Sri Lanka. China had made this clear to the Sri Lanka's ruling coalition partner, Janata Vimukti Perumana (JVP), when the party leaders traveled to Beijing in 2005 to petition the Chinese to move into Trincomalee. The US is already overextended in international hot spots would prefer that India get more active in the island, now that the USSR has unraveled. India is no more a junior partner of the Soviet Union, and hence would not threaten US vital interests as proxy for a Communist empire. Only Pakistan, which is today living in the past and still dreaming of an equation with India, has tried to intervene; but it lacks the background to strike a chord of empathy with Sri Lanka's masses.

The question is how the Indian intervention has to be structured so as to not repeat the follies of 1987-89. For this structuring, India has to clearly set the parameters of the scope and limits of the intervention as follows:

First, India should never allow the LTTE to head or be a part of any future regional or national government in Sri Lanka as long as Prabhakaran, the LTTE supremo, and Pottu Amman the second in command, are not handed over to India for concluding the incomplete trial in the Rajiv Gandhi assassination case. Let us not forget that the LTTE advocate had told the Supreme Court of India, while arguing the appeal of the 26 LTTE persons sentenced to death by the trial court, that Prabhakaran had ordered Rajiv Gandhi's assassination because he "had wanted to teach Rajiv Gandhi a lesson for IPKF atrocities" and that he had also "wanted to prevent him from coming back as Prime Minister."

If we in India have any patriotism left, then we must resolve that India shall not rest till the LTTE supremo is taught a lesson for Rajiv Gandhi's assassination and that Prabhakaran does not ever come to legitimate power for this perfidy against India. No foreign force can dare to think that the leader of a billion people can be "taught a lesson" nor have the hubris to decide who should or should not become the Prime Minister of India.

Even if the Congress Party (of which Rajiv Gandhi was President up to the time of his assassination) for some obscure compulsion shows scant interest today in bringing to book the LTTE's supremo Vellupillai Prabhakaran for this crime against the nation, patriotic Indians cannot forget either Rajiv's martyrdom or LTTE's perfidy. India has to fix Prabhakaran some day by bringing him to justice, or otherwise, creating *justice on him* for the lack of respect for India's sovereignty that the assassination of Rajiv Gandhi represents.

Second, no Indian intervention should exclude Colombo from its scope. That was the fatal error that Rajiv Gandhi had made the last time when IPKF was sent. He trusted that the Sinhala politicians would be grateful and helpful. But the Sinhala mind has been poisoned by the British concocted history of an Aryan-Dravidian divide, by which the short wiry haired dark-skinned Sinhalas see themselves as long lost relatives of the blond-haired blue-eyed Europeans living 15,000 kilometres away, rather than as cousins of all Indians, 35 kilometres across the Palk Straits. Thus, betraying or ditching the "low Dravidians" is permissible! If Sinhalas give up this inane adherence to Aryan supremacy, India would welcome them as brothers and sisters.

Hence, if India is to intervene, then it must post two division of the Indian Army in Colombo, and a squadron of the Indian Air Force in a cantonment area of Colombo. This is the only way we can ensure that our soldiers are not killed in vain, and that we are not once more victims of the ingratitude and perfidy of the Sinhala politicians. And if the Sinhala Government is reluctant to agree to these preconditions, we should unhesitatingly use other methods of persuasion as the "eldest brother" of the South Asian region, to make Sri Lanka agree. India cannot afford to allow Sri Lanka to internationalize our backyard or waffle on this issue anymore.

Third, there are only three viable alternative solutions to the ethnic problem in the island. *The first solution* is to adopt an Indian type quasi-federal Constitution for a united sovereign Sri Lanka. This is the *minimal* demand of Tamils. *The second is* the partition of the island to create an independent sovereign state of Eelam. This, however, at present, would mean India has to make a long-term commitment to sustain the survival of Eelam—or risk, as in the case of Bangladesh, Eelam becoming a future base of our enemies. On the face of it, this is unacceptable to us. The *third* alternative is the merger of the island with India. This is the maximal demand of any Indian. Of the three alternatives, the first is the least painful for the Sri Lanka Government and it is feasible today; but time is rapidly running out for its acceptance by Tamils. In 1991 the Tamils would have enthusiastically agreed; but as time now passes, this alternative is becoming less and less acceptable to Tamils. There is also a danger that this solution is a stepping-stone to the second alternative solution, i.e. the creation of an independent Eelam. It could then pave the way for the LTTE to return with the help of the ISI of Pakistan or other anti-Indian forces. Hence, for the foreseeable future, Eelam is ruled out as an option, since this second solution is wholly fraught with danger for Indian integrity and national security. Given the current "Dravidian" movement parties' dependence for money from the LTTE (which the LTTE has plenty of from the ISI-sponsored narcotics trade), Eelam in the island can lead to a Kashmir type situation in Tamil Nadu later. Thus, India, for its own national interests has to view it as the least desirable alternative solution, and rule it out as an option.

India's most preferred solution is the first alternative solution of a quasi-federal Constitution. And if that is not acceptable, then the only feasible alternative from our point of view is the third solution of integrating Sri Lanka with India, either first by confederating like in Europe or by outright merger, as was the case with Sikkim. A continued impasse in the current Sri Lanka crisis would create the dynamics for India to initiate the process for a peaceful merger of the island with the Indian mainland.

What thus is clear today is that a unitary state of Sri Lanka is a dead letter. The Buddhists monks wrote its epitaph when they recently acknowledged that they had wrongly opposed the IPKF, and now want it back. *My friend, the late Rajiv Gandhi, has been vindicated at last.*

Therefore, India must oppose the present Norwegian orchestrated "peace dialogue" of the Sri Lanka government with the LTTE—which talks could end up legitimizing the terrorist outfit and making the ban on the LTTE in Indian meaningless.

Despite the murder of their Foreign Minister Kadirgamar and the attempted murder of their then President Chandrika Kumaratunga by the LTTE, the Sri Lankan authorities appear to be suffering from the "Stockholm Syndrome," of capitulating to their tormentors, by agreeing to talk with them at a moment's notice. Thus they are wholly incompetent to deal with the murderous LTTE. The Sri Lanka President's first reaction after the murder of Foreign Minister Kadirgamar was that the island government would not suspend the so-called peace talks with the killers, a further indication of the same tragic Stockholm syndrome that seems to petrify them.

Sri Lanka thus seems a crumbling failed state that has lost its collective nerve to combat and confront the terror of the LTTE.

If the Sinhala majority really want to rid the island of the LTTE and restore Sinhala-Tamil amity, then they should force their government to unilaterally announce the adoption of a quasi-federal Constitution, much like India's, to replace the present unitary one. Then India, without reservation can help the Sri Lankans to combat the LTTE. But we cannot wait around for the waffling Sinhala politicians to make up their minds, since this delay tantamounts to strengthening the LTTE and helping it to recover it's losses during the "cease-fire" period.

Thanks to some quiet diplomacy from India, the Sri Lanka politicians have at last moved forward to come to a consensus on how to deal with the LTTE by political counter-moves that win over the silent majority amongst the Tamils. The two major opposing parties the SFLP and the UNP have come together to sign a "MoU" on 23 October 2006 to resolve issues of the current Sri Lankan crisis and establish peace by mutual consultations and agreement. This is a good harbinger of the future, and the international community should therefore support the initiative.

However, these two parties should make efforts to bring on board the JVP by accommodating the party's two main conditions: (1) that the Norwegian interlocutors be de-recognized as mediators and sent home; and (2) that the Cease-fire Agreement (CFA) be scrapped. Both conditions are eminently reasonable. The Norwegians are a bored people who keep themselves busy by being political busybodies. They have never been impartial, and have been amenable to non-political inducements from the LTTE. Much of what they say sounds inane or one-sided. As for the CFA, it is just a piece of paper. How can a sovereign government have a cease-fire agreement with an internationally banned terrorist organization that has killed so many Sri Lankan leaders? As I have stated, India will not accept any solution in which the LTTE is a part whatever the government may say publicly. As stated earlier, the *LTTE is a part of the problem, and cannot be a part of any solution.*

Thus India has a national security imperative and an unavoidable moral responsibility to get involved to free the island of Sri Lanka from the LTTE's treacherous terror. If for nothing else this must be done to secure our own environment and punish those who seek to overawe our people with terror after receiving our hospitality and calling India their "mother country." It is our obligation to Sri Lanka to rid it of the problem that LTTE represents.

I see five specific basis for this obligations:

First, India had trained the LTTE in the 1980s and created the Frankenstein monster. Hence, India has to atone for it by taking actions to disband and unravel the LTTE.

Second, despite enjoying India's hospitality for years, and after welcoming the Indo-Sri Lanka Agreement in 1967, the LTTE betrayed India by killing more than a thousand Indian army personnel of the IPKF sent to the island to enforce the said agreement. The betrayal and loss of lives of our valiant jawans have to be avenged to keep up the morale of the Indian armed forces.

Third, as the Home Ministry 2005 Annual Report to Parliament quoted above states, LTTE has been targeting pro-Indian Sri Lanka politicians and assassinating them. For the assassination of Rajiv Gandhi, an Indian trial court has declared accused number one Prabhakaran as a proclaimed offender, and the Interpol has issued a Red Corner Notice for apprehending him. Thus India is obligated to search for Prabhakaran and to teach the LTTE a lesson in a language they will understand, and to immobilize them enough to deter them in the future from engaging in any murderous and terrorist activities against India and Indian interests.

Fourth, the LTTE interferes in the internal affairs of India by financing stooge Indian political parties, by providing training to Indian militant and extremist organizations, and by extending insurgency infrastructure to bandits such as Veerappan and his forest gang. It also launders the black money of Indian politicians through it's illegal Eelam Bank in the Jaffna area. India cannot allow such erosion of law and order within it's own borders.

Fifth, the LTTE is part of the international terror network of Al Qaeda and is aided by the ISI of Pakistan to smuggle narcotics into India, circulate fake currency notes to buy medicines and diesel, smuggle out antiques to Europe, and engage in passport fabrication, and hawala operations. As senior RAW (India's foreign intelligence agency) official B. Rama has disclosed, the then Prime Minister of Pakistan, Nawaz Sharif, was shocked when the US brought the ISI-LTTE link to his notice. This has been re-affirmed recently in *Times of India* 17 June 2005 in an article which identified Koyalapatnam village in Tamil Nadu as the "centre for LTTE and ISI."

The question thus is: *To discharge those obligations what should India do?* Obviously, we cannot depend on the Sri Lanka governments of today or of the near future to be militarily able to bring the LTTE to book. Sri Lankan political parties have been either capitulationist in the face of terrorism or chauvinist. Both these attitudes help the LTTE. President Rajapakse's agreement with JVP during the last elections was that his government would defend the present failed unitary constitution. If this is not given up, then the Tamils will remain squeezed between the devil (LTTE) and the deep sea (Sinhala chauvinists). Hence, India has to initiate action to meet its own obligations, and it can expect no worthwhile cooperation from the Sinhala parties.

The first move India should make is to initiate action and steps to revive the hunt for those of the LTTE who have to be booked and prosecuted under Indian law. This includes the LTTE supremo Prabhakaran and his sidekick Pottu Amman, and whoever else in India has tried to help the LTTE to escape the arm of India's law enforcement.

In 1998, as noted earlier, Parliament had set up under the CBI a "multidisciplinary monitoring agency" [MDMA] to hunt for these wanted persons. But the NDA Government waffled after it was set up and failed to pursue the matter. The present UPA Government has been worse on this issue. It has been wobbling on the question of extradition of Prabhakaran. [According *The Hindu* of 30 December 1998, appended here, Ms Gandhi railed to raise the issue when she met President Kumaratunge]. It is soft on other issues as well. The Congress Party saw no wrong in forming a political alliance with those pro-LTTE in Tamil Nadu who defend the LTTE assassination of Rajiv Gandhi. When Sri Lanka President Chandrika Kumaratunga came to India, the UPA Government agreed to let the LTTE be a party in the Tsunami relief work and have its share in the $3 billion international aid commitment. It was only after the US declined to provide the funds if LTTE was

A major landmark, says Chandrika

By K.K. Katyal

NEW DELHI, 29 December. Taking a highly positive view of the present state of her country's relations with India, the Sri Lankan President, Mrs Chandrika Kumaratunga, has commended the agreement on free trade as a major landmark, representing a break with the past. In a talk with a group of media-persons at Rashtrapati Bhavan today, she said the agreement became possible because of the political will, both in India and Sri Lanka, which, to her, was the most important factor. She was, however, not unconscious of the possible difficulties ahead and as she put it: "I do not expect to walk on a bed of roses."

It was clear from her replies—and the occasional comments of the Sri Lankan Foreign Minister, Mr Lakshman Kadirgamar, who, too, was present—that she was fully satisfied with the agreement. Asked whether Sri Lanka could have got a better deal, she remarked: "There has to be give and take. The agreement is allright." It was her impression that the leadership of the main Opposition party in Sri Lanka would support it.

Mrs Kumaratunga regarded the annexures to the agreement as a routine affair, while seeking to dispel the impression that these documents contained conditions and riders. "The annexures are going to contain details (which cannot be incorporated in the main agreement), not conditions," she said.

The recent nuclear tests, she said in reply to a question, had not affected her country's relationship with India. Sri Lanka did express its concern to both India and Pakistan but was assured that they did not intend to go farther. "We expressed our opinion but we go on," she said, impliedly suggesting that the assurances were considered satisfactory.

She was asked whether the presence of the MDMK (with its pro-LTTE leanings) in the BJP-led coalition worried her. Mrs Kumaratunga did not appear familiar with the nomenclature of the party and inquired of the questioner what exactly he had in mind. "This provides an answer," Mr Kadirgamar quipped, as she added: "It is not a serious problem."

Apart from bilateral matters, the questioners focussed on the ethnic crisis—the army operations against the LTTE, the fate of the devolution package, the Government's overall approach to the search for a solution. "The LTTE must agree to certain conditions," if the dialogue were to be resumed, she said, while emphasising that "we want an early end to the ethnic problem," Asked about her views of the role of facilitators and mediators, she gave a general reply—"There are accepted norms for facilitators and mediators. This is how we expect it to be." Will South African President, Mr Nelson Mandela, be acceptable? "We had many offers from different countries and international organisations, "We will decide when the time arises," was her reply. Has not the time, come after 15 years of strife and 50,000 casualties? "Time was (there) a long ago I feel it is time that the LTTE must agree to certain conditions." She did not seek facilitation from the Prime Minister, Mr Atal Behari Vajpayee—this was her reply to another query.

Had not the political package been delayed because of the lack of consensus among the Sinhala sections? According to her, there were two aspects. One, the majority of the Sinhala people had accepted the package but the leadership of the major Opposition parties had not. Two, the Government did not have two-thirds majority in Parliament to amend the constitution (for the purpose of incorporating the package) and, as such, could not proceed because of the intransigence and obstinacy of the opposition.

Explaining the complicated nature of the constitution which did not give two-thirds majority to her party even after its win in 80 per cent seats, she made the oft-repeated point that "we have to think of other solutions. While choosing not to spell out the details she agreed with a questioner that referendum could be one of the steps. What she had in mind was a "devious but a democratic" route. The Government, according to her, had the moral and political right to do so because of her party's performance in the elections.

Don't you think you should give another chance to the LTTE supremo, Prabhakaran, to prove his bona fides? "Does he have bona fides. How do you propose we ask him for it?" Was her counter-query. She justified curbs on the local Press because of its misuse of (the freedom) in the present emergency situation but clarified that there was no censorship on the foreign media. There was no plan to shelve military operations, she said, denying reports to that effect.

The rehabilitation of Jaffna was fairly satisfactory but was "not progressing as we would like it," because of the absence of the land link, India, she told another questioner, was helping in the rehabilitation of Jaffna.

Had Mrs Sonia Gandhi, whom she met today, raised the question of extradition of those responsible for Rajiv Gandhi's assassination? "No." What was the progress with extradition? "If you can catch them for us, we will immediately extradite them.

Later in the evening it was learnt that Mrs Kumaratunga had decided to extend her stay in India by a day till Wednesday.

Official sources said the Sri Lankan leader had expressed her desire to stay on to complete her engagements which had been deferred due to her busy schedule.

The Union Home Minister, Mr L.K. Advani, would call on her tomorrow morning to discuss issues of mutual interest.

Hindu, 30 December 1998

involved, that Ms Chandrika Kumaratunga was stopped from disbursing money through the LTTE.

The time is now at hand to energize the MDMA, to get moving to apprehend the wanted criminals and bring them to book. For this, India may have to dispatch a squad of commando force to Jaffna, a force that India has had trained in Israel since 1994 in batches. These commandos, with the cover of helicopter gunships and GPS-satellite guided, can easily locate where Prabhakaran is hiding and smoke him out.

Second, India must assist and nurture the democratic elements in the Sri Lankan Tamil population, those that have demonstrated the capacity to stand up to the LTTE such as S.C. Chandrahasan, and breakaway LTTE group that had opposed Rajiv Gandhi's assassination, viz the Karuna group and current Sri Lanka Minister Douglas Devanando to form a non-violent and democratic alternative to work out with the Sinhala majority the federal or quasi-federal constitution that would serve the purpose of power sharing.

Third, there are LTTE sleeper cells in Delhi, Mumbai, Bangalore and other cities of Indian, stooges of the LTTE in political parties, media and government, who have to be identified, and imprisoned under a new anti-terrorist law. These cells work under anonymity to sabotage any patriotic effort made to nail the LTTE. At present, terrorists of various hues are active in 29 of the 35 States and union territories of India. The common link of all these terrorists is the LTTE-ISI nexus because Jaffna is close by and Pakistan is a sanctuary for all these terrorists. (See the news item in *Times of India,* 7 June 2005 appended with other news items.) Hence, one day all of sudden these terrorists and LTTE sleeper cells may coordinate and cause a huge bloody incident by which India's recent international repute for reforms, fast growth, and IT development, could all go up in smoke. We have to guard against such contingencies by preemptive action.

Pakistan's secret state

When the Twin Towers were attacked on 9 September 2001, Pakistan's then ISI chief Gen Mahmoud Ahmed was visiting the US. Soon after his return, Gen Pervez Musharraf was forced to take the historic decision of turning his back on the Taliban that the ISI had created and nurtured for close to a decade.

Ahmed, along with a handful of other ISI men and religious leaders, was dispatched to Kandahar in Afghanistan to convince Mullah Omar to give up Osama bin Laden to the US. But according to later reports, Ahmed joined the religious leaders in exhorting the Taliban leader to continue his jihad against America, which would be supported by sections of Pakistan's establishment (read ISI).

The best comment about Pakistan's infamous ISI came from a former Pakistan high commissioner to UK, Wajid Shamsul Hasan. "It's a state within a state," he said. "Pakistan's foreign policy has been run by the ISI rather than the foreign office." In many ways, it explains why three years after Pakistan cut off its ties with the Taliban, sections within the ISI continue to maintain close links.

Besides, as Stephen Cohen of Brookings Institution then pointed out, "You can't develop ties over 10 or 15 years and then cut them off instantly. It's a big bureaucracy and changing its direction will take a while."

The Directorate for Inter-Services Intelligence (ISI) was founded in 1948 by a British army officer, Maj Gen R. Cawthome, then deputy chief of staff in the Pakistan Army. Field Marshal Ayub Khan, president of Pakistan in the 1950s, expanded the role of ISI in safeguarding Pakistan's interests, monitoring opposition politicians, and sustaining military rule in Pakistan.

Today, scholars say ISI has moved beyond the scope of the army leadership, though Musharraf has stated that he is in complete control of the intelligence organisation.

This degree of independence has meant that there has been no real supervision of the ISI, and corruption, narcotics and big money have all come into play, further complicating the political scenario. Drug money has been used by ISI to finance not only the Afghanistan war, but also the proxy war against India in Punjab and Kashmir.

According to Indian and international intelligence analysts, the ISI supplies weapons, training, advice and planning assistance to terrorists in Punjab and Kashmir, as well as the separatist movements in north-east India. It's reported to be operating training camps near the Bangladesh border to train ULFA cadres and supply them with equipment for terror activities. Other groups include the National Security Council of Nagaland (NSCN), People's Liberation Army (PLA) and North-East Students' Organisation (NESO).

The ISI is said to have intensified its activities in Andhra Pradesh, Karanataka and Kerala. In Andhra Pradesh, the Ittehadul Musalmeen and the Hizbul Mujahideen are reported to be involved in subversive activities promoted by ISI. And *Koyalapattinam, a village in Tamil Nadu, is said to be the common centre of operations of ISI and Sri Lanka's LTTE.*

Pakistan is overtly playing for peace with India. So are these activities of the ISI sanctioned by the state?

Times of India, 1 June 2005

Pakistan-LTTE Link Seen

COLOMBO (UNI) — The United States and Britain advised Pakistan against attempts to use the Liberation Tigers of Tamil Eelam, the rebel Sri Lankan organization, to destabilize South India, according to an authoritative Lankan source.

Islamabad was warned against involvement with the Tamil militants, following intelligence reports of a growing nexus between it and the militants, the source said.

Denied Terrorist Links

"They told us they had asked Pakistan not to get involved with the LTTE, and we also took up the matter with Pakistan, but they denied any links with the terrorists," the source added.

It was not known at what level the U.S. and Britain had taken up the matter with Islamabad. The source said their "advice" to Islamabad followed reports that senior LTTE leader Sathasivam Krishnakumar, better known as Kittu, had gone to Pakistan on arms-buying missions.

Kittu's suicide after his arms-laden ship was surrounded by Indian naval vessels off the Madras coast in January last year dealt a severe blow to the growing nexus between Islamabad and the rebels, diplomatic observers believed.

'Rogue Operation'

The plan to use the LTTE to whip up trouble in South India was part of what an observer called a "rogue operation" by Pakistan's Inter-Services Intelligence.

"It was a minimal investment with maximum potential for mischief," the source said, adding that Pakistan's foreign policy operated on the principle that an "enemy's enemy is my friend."

Pakistan probably wanted to use the LTTE and Colombo to antagonize India, the observers said, adding that its plans could have also upset the security situation in Sri Lanka.

There was enough evidence that Kittu had been "flitting in and out" of Pakistan to buy arms, they said.

"The biggest illegal arms market in the sub-continent is in Pakistan and the authorities there had just to close their eyes to what was going on," said another source, who declined to be identified.

India Abroad, 10 July 1995

Tigers deny mafia link

Colombo, 11 Febuary: Sri Lanka's Tamil Tiger rebels, accused by the European Commission's envoy to south Asia of possible links to organised crime, have vehemently denied ties with the mafia.

Ms Francine Henrich, stressing the European Union's solidarity with Sri Lanka's efforts to stem the rebels' separatist campaign, told reporters here there was "some indication" the militants were involved in drug-trafficking and with the mafia. The LTTE, in a letter sent to Ms Henrich from the northern Jaffna peninsula, said her comments were "grossly misleading and highly slanderous." "We wish to state categorically that we have no links with the mafia nor are we involved in drug-trafficking," the LTTE's head of political section Mr S.P. Thamilselvan, said. The LTTE has been accused by the government in the bombing of the Central Bank on 31 January. (*Reuter*)

Asian Age, 12 February 1996

The time is at hand for India to effectively contribute to the war against terrorism and for promotion of democracy by targeting the LTTE sincerely and effectively in the larger national interest of security and national integrity. There is today a window of opportunity due to international consensus against the LTTE, and we must seize it now.

The bottom line of the current situation of crisis in Sri Lanka is that *we have to intervene.* We do not intervene for the Sinhala or the Tamils, but in the interest of our national security. The question is how that intervention has to be structured so as not to repeat the follies the past.

Hence, we Indians have to take stock now and decide what to do to remove the fault line in our policy towards the LTTE, and thus secure our geographical neighbourhood. The LTTE, which could be legitimized by the Sri Lanka Government aided by inane Norwegian facilitation, will be a menace not only to Sri Lanka's integrity, but also to India's national security. (Since the Tigers have links with India's terrorists such as the Maoists and ULFA, and with the ISI of Pakistan and even Al Qaeda and with separatist Indian political parties). Even Bandit Veerappan functioned as a conduit for the LTTE. Besides the LTTE has ferried narcotics through India as the media reports appended here shows.

Thus India has a national security imperative and an unavoidable moral obligation to get involved to help rid the island of Sri Lanka of the LTTE's treacherous terror, if for nothing else but to secure our own environment and to punish those who seek to overawe the people with terror.

The time is at hand for India to effectively contribute to the war against terrorism and for the promotion of democracy, by targeting the LTTE sincerely and effectively in the larger interest of security and national integrity. No Indian option to intervene can be exercised without this pre-condition.

57 Years of Conflict

1949	Indian Tamil planation workers were disenfranchised.
1956	Solomon Bandaranaike was elected on a wave of Sinhalese nationalism. Sinhala was made sole official language, thereby Sinhalese and Buddhist feeling bolstering.
1971	In the Sinhalese Marxist uprising, led by students and activists, Buddhism was given primary place, thereby antagonising the Tamil minority.
1976	As tensions increase in Tamil-dominated areas of north and east, the Liberation Tigers of Tamil Eelam (LTTE) was formed.
1983	13 soldiers were killed in an LTTE ambush thereby sparking anti-Tamil riots wherein, it is estimated several hundred Tamils were killed.
1987	Government forces pushed LTTE back to the northern city of Jaffna. Government signed accords creating new councils for Tamil areas in north and east and an Indian peace-keeping force was deployed.
1990	Indian troops left after getting bogged down in fighting in the north. Violence between the Sri Lankan army and LTTE escalated.
1991	LTTE assassinated former Indian PM Rajiv Gandhi in Sriperumbudur.
1993	President Premadasa was killed in an LTTE bomb attack. In 1994, President Kumaratunga came to power pledging to end war and peace talks with LTTE were held.
1995	Peace talks collapsed and LTTE resumed its bombing campaign.

1999	President Kumaratunga was wounded in a bomb attack at an election rally. She was re-elected President.
Feb. 2002	Government and Tamil Tiger rebels signed a permanent ceasefire agreement, paving the way for talks.
Dec. 2002	At peace talks in Norway, government and rebels agreed to share power. Under the deal, minority Tamils would have autonomy in the mainly Tamil-speaking north and east.
Nov. 2003	President Kumaratunga dismissed three ministers, and suspended parliament. (She had been at odds with government over peace process).
March 2004	Renegade Tamil Tiger commander, Karuna, led a split in the rebel movement.
April 2004	Early general elections were held amid a political power struggle. Mahinda Rajapakse was sworn in as Prime Minister.
Aug. 2005	A State of emergency was declared after Foreign Minister Lakshman Kadirgamar was assassinated.
April 2006	A suicide bomber attacked the main military compound in Colombo, killing at least eight people. The military launched air strikes on Tamil Tiger targets.
16 Oct.	When it faced increased pressure from Lankan 2006 military forces and was forced more and more into a defensive mode. The LTTE perpetrated the brutal suicide bombing at Habarana, north-east of Colombo. This killed 103 Sri Lankan sailors

	on Monday, signating the LTTE's return to its signature style of inflicting violence through guerrilla tactics.
17 Oct. 2006	The Sri Lankan Supreme Court's judgement was pronounced, annulling the merger of north and east Sri Lanka. This sets the clock back to the 1980s when the Indian government took the initiative to persuade Sri Lanka to agree to the concept of a historical Tamil homeland and to consider the 13th amendment which aimed to devolve powers to Tamils. The judgment is a set back to moderate Tamil groups who have espoused joining the main stream under a united Sri Lanka.

The heroin trail through India

Working through third parties, the LTTE may never be directly implicated in the narcotics traffic, writes Nirupama Subramanian

The motor launch was hugging the coast near Tuticorin on the Tamil Nadu coast when it was challenged by an Indian Customs patrol. Immediately the launch, which bore. Sri Lankan markings, made for the high seas. But its escape bid was abortive. Customs officials boarded the boat to discover plastic sacks full of heroin—a whopping 52.8 kg. The consignment was headed for Sri Lanka.

This happened last fortnight and was the second haul of heroin in Tamil Nadu in a month and the fifth in 14 months. One other heroin seizure was made at Bangalore and:

- In August 1998, customs officials at Trichy arrested a Sri Lankan man carrying 27 kg at the international airport.
- In March 1999, the Department of Revenue Intelligence seized 28 kg from a Sri Lankan in Chennai.
- In April 1999, the Narcotics Control Bureau caught an Indian with 16 kg of the same drug in Chennai.
- In June 1999, the NCB arrested a Sri Lankan and an Indian with 10.6 kg of heroin in Bangalore.
- In October 1999, customs officials caught an Indian with 10 kg of the narcotic at Dindigul in Tamil Nadu.

According to the Police Narcotics Division of Sri Lanka, about 50 kg of heroin is seized annually as it enters the country. Sri Lankan police admit that the island is being used as a major transit point for the drug. Its journey begins in Afghanistan and Pakistan and it traverses the length of India before entering Sri Lanka, from where it heads for Western Europe.

"Earlier, traffickers used the overland Balkan route to Europe. But with the unrest in that region, the Tamil Nadu-Sri Lanka route has become more attractive," says C.L. Ratnayake, director of Sri Lanka's Police Narcotics Division.

Ratnayake says that traffickers chose the most "tedious and non-obvious" routes to their final destination in order to avoid detection. The larger consignments come by sea from the Tamil Nadu coast, particularly the area around Tuticorin, and land on Sri Lanka's north-western coast. While there have been regular seizures of the drug as it enters Sri Lanka, there have been few hauls at the exit points, and none in the last year.

Indian police sources said that besides members of the Indian underworld, a few Sri Lankans living in India, with connections to the underworld on the island, are also in the trade. Narcotics police have under their surveillance some Chennai-based Sri Lankans who control a network of couriers who carry the drugs into Sri Lanka.

"The deals and transactions are still made in Delhi and Bombay, after which the drugs flow southward," said an Indian police officer. Earlier, the consignments were transported overland across India. But increasingly, this is done through domestic Indian flights on which security is less stringent.

Drug trafficking has created strong links between the Indian and Sri Lankan underworld, a fact that became evident after the recent arrest of heroin boss Kuda Noor by the Sri Lankan Crime Detection Bureau. Indian police said reverberations of the arrest were felt across the straits, in Tamil Nadu's underworld.

The history of smuggling by sea across the Palk Straits meant that the networks were already in place. The common ethnicity and the huge influx into India of Tamil refugees from Sri Lanka after 1983 seems to have facilitated the business. Inevitably, there is suspicion that the Liberation Tigers of Tamil Eelam (LTTE), the group fighting for a separate homeland in north-eastern Sri Lanka, is responsible for the upsurge of narcotics-related activity in this region.

The group seems to have a bottomless treasury and is almost as well-equipped as the Sri Lankan army. But it has been extremely difficult to pin anything as dirty as drugs on the avowedly puritanical LTTE. At a recent international conference on narco-terrorism held in Colombo, a Canadian police officer described the link between the LTTE and the narcotics trade as "hazy" at best. "It is the most logical assumption to make that the LTTE is involved in narcotics, but there is no evidence," an Indian police officer told this newspaper.

On 7 January Sriram, 36, was shot outside a farmhouse in West Delhi. A Sri Lankan, he had been running a drugs racket. While the killers remain untraced, three Sri Lankan associates of Sriram were arrested, who revealed that Sriram was an "LTTE-trained commando." Later, underworld boss Ashwin Naik, who was caught trying to flee India across the Bangladesh border, corroborated the story.

Delhi Police then announced they had evidence in their possession that could, for the "first time," connect the LTTE with the illegal trade in narcotics. They pointed to the fact that Sriram had once supplied an Uzi to Ashwin Naik's gangster brother Amar, as evidence that the LTTE was pedding drugs for arms.

However, this was not the first time that the LTTE-drugs link had surfaced. Since 1984, soon after many Sri Lankan Tamils left their country to seek asylum in the West, several have been arrested the world over for drug-running. The arrested men claimed connections with many of the militant groups that had mushroomed in Sri Lanka at that time.

In a few cases, police said there was evidence to suggest they were members of the LTTE. But there never was independent evidence to establish the link conclusively, or to show how the LTTE benefited from these operations.

Secondly, it has never been proved that any of the Tamils arrested so far for drug-running were affiliated with the LTTE. In only two instances has the link come close to being established: in the mid-eighties, a western journalist who contacted the LTTE in a European capital posing as a drug baron wrote that it had responded positively.

Interpol recently revealed that the LTTE's Paris "in-charge" till some time ago, Velumailyum Manoharan alias Mano, had a heroin conviction. The suspicion that he was acting for the LTTE arose after a report that Velupillai Prabhakaran had authorised a monthly payment to his family while he served time.

In Sriram's case, Tamil Nadu police have no record of him being a member of any Tamil millitant outfit. He arrived in India in 1988, one of the thousands of Sri Lankan Tamils who took refuge in Tamil Nadu at that time.

Sources among former militant groups in Sri Lanka harbour little doubt that the group profits from narcotics-related activities. But to establish its direct involvement in the traffic is next to impossible.

"Those involved in the racket may not even be aware that they are working for the LTTE," said one former militant. It is believed that in order to maintain its image of fierce puritanism, the LTTE lets others do the dirty work, demanding only a share of the profits.

In all these years of pursuing the LTTE, the Sri Lankan security forces too have found no evidence to directly associate it with the narcotics business. It is suspected that the drugs trade could be linked to the human smuggling racket in Sri Lanka, through which hundreds of Sri Lankan Tamils are sent illegally to the West every year. Sriram's first venture in India was in fact a false passport business.

Sundaralingam, a 23-year-old Jaffna youth who was taken into custody in Colombo in a drug bust—on a tip-off provided by two Indians held for bringing heroin into Sri Lanka from Chennai—was also said to be running an "agency," Tamil shorthand for immigration racket.

Police said they were looking for LTTE links. However, in this case as in others, everything that could connect the LTTE to narcotics is still in the realm of suspicion and, given the dark complexity of the drug chain, may forever remain so.

The Indian Express, 3 November 1999

TN a major conduit for Lanka-bound drugs

G.C. Shekhar, Chennai, 1 October

Tamil Nadu has emerged as the single biggest conduit for drugs going into Sri Lanka with increased seizures by the authorities. However, there has been no evidence to suggest the LTTE's hand in the drug racket though most operators are Sri Lankan Muslims who also engage Lankan Tamil refugees settled in the state.

According to NCB sources an estimated 10,000 kg of heroin might be smuggled into the island state annually to cater to over 2 lakh addicts which is said to be at least twice as large as in India. The heroin that gets into Sri Lanka, mostly through Negombo, north of Colombo, is a mix of both Indian and Pakistani origin.

"The preference in Lanka appears to be for Indian-made heroin coming from poppy growing states like MP, UP and Rajasthan. Mandsaur district in MP has emerged as one of the largest cartels," pointed out a senior official of the state CID which arrested two operators from Mandsaur while transporting 10 kg of heroin in July 2000. Similarly a lorry with MP registration carrying 20 kilos of heroin in June was traced to Zubeida, the sister of known drug king Mohammad Shafi of Mandsaur. Similarly out of 150 kilos of heroin seized by NCB in the South in the last one year almost 100 kgs came from Mandsaur.

According to official sources Sri Lankan operators now go directly to Madhya Pradesh to strike deals with local heroin producers, who manufacture the drug in clandestine labs after procuring excess poppy yields from local farmers at exorbitant prices. The heroin packets are then concealed in lorries that carry other general goods to the coast especially Tuticorin port.

In fact many Lankan operators, instead of advancing money for a consignment enter into partnership with producers in MP. Once the heroin is sold in Lanka the producer in Mandsaur gets his cut through the hawala route, the official disclosed. Ever since NCB and CID police in Tamil Nadu started to crack down on lorries coming from MP, the operators now enter Tamil Nadu through Karnataka with Belgaum emerging as a favourite stocking point before the drug is moved to the TN coast in lorries with non-MP registration.

NCB sources also reveal that the Lankan operators used carriers to take heroin through scheduled flights. Another favourite destination for heroin smugglers in India is Milan in Italy, where security is said to be quite lax. "Milan has become a preferred entry point in Europe for drugs," said an NCB officer.

What has baffled authorities is that they have not yet got any evidence to link the LTTE to any of the drug operations though most operators are Tamil speaking Lankan Muslims who also draft Lankan Tamils living in India for their operations. Also the fact that Sri Lankan authorities have not reported any major seizures from passengers going from Colombo to Europe or Canada, has punctured the popular theory that the Tigers smuggle drugs to buy weapons. Another theory has it that the LTTE might be moving all its drug consignments through the sea considering the lax coastal security in the island nation.

"Ten thousand kilos of heroin into such a small nation looks abnormal by any proportion. It should be going out through other means," said a senior police officer familiar with the drug trade.

Hindustan Times, 2 October 2000

LTTE, ISI reaping bumper opium harvest in Mandsaur

HT Correspondent, Indore, 1 October

A Bumper opium crop this year in the Mandsaur area of Madhya Pradesh has sent alarm bells ringing in the state intelligence setup. It is revealed that a bulk of the produce is getting into the hands of heroin smugglers who have found a new route—down South from where, the state police fear, the drug is bartered for arms meant for the Liberation Tigers of Tamil Eelam (LTTE) and Pakistan's Inter Services Intelligence.

Police sources said the Inter Services Intelligence and the LTTE were sponsoring the drug trade.

The annual illegal trade is worth nearly Rs. 250 to 300 crore in the Malwa region. This year, however, the estimate may be grossly under-estimated owing to the bumper opium crop in the Mandsaur-Neemuch belt.

Over the last few years, Indore has emerged as a major transit point for the transportation of drugs to both Mumbai and Chennai.

Mandsaur Superintendent of Police Ajay Kumar Sharma told *The Hindustan Times* that though the exact money going into purchase of illegal arms by the foreign agencies is yet to be ascertained, the district police have seized large quantities of illegal opium and other drugs, and expects record seizures this year.

According to the police, the main reason for the Mandsaur drugs to be transported to the southern region is that North India was flooded with heroin, brown sugar and smack from Afghanistan, which is generally of high quality. This had made the market less lucrative for the Malwa-Mewar region produce.

The Mandsaur Police had submitted a report six months back to the state police headquarters stating that local traders were using international terrorist organisations as a conduit to market their drugs. The police based their assessment on the information collected during interrogation of those arrested for involvement in the drug trade.

The narco-terrorism link came to light some time back when one Sohrab Pathan, with links in Gujarat, was arrested at Jhiraniya in Ujjain district.

According to the police records, Chhota Dawood, a resident of Pratapgarh, near Mandsaur is a big name in the smuggling world. Chhota Dawood has links with D Group of Dawood Ibrahim and Latif, a Gujarat smuggler.

Mandsaur police had nabbed a Pakistani citizen Muzaffar Ali with drugs.

In the same way, the Chittorgarh police had arrested three members of the Jammu Kashmir Liberation Front (JKLF) with drugs from Mandsaur.

Hindustan Times, 2 October 2000

LTTE ran training camp for Naxals in Gadchiroli

by Pittala Ravinder

Karimnagar (AP)—A six-member team of the LTTE has imparted training in the use of sophisticated weaponry to about 300 select members of the People's War Group of Naxalites.

The training "course" between 9 May and 2 June took place in the dense forests of Gadchiroli of bordering Maharashtra, according to PWG squad members who attended the camp conducted under the watchful eyes of top PWG leaders like Muppala Laxman Rao alias Ganapathi, Nalla Adi Reddy alias Shyam and Mallojula Koteshwar Rao alias Prahalad.

According to the PWG members who preferred anonymity, they were trained in the use of rocket-launchers and the LTTE militants are stated to have promised to provide the Naxalites 100 such launchers.

After the training, the PWG decided to constitute "suicide squads" whose members will be ....

Indian Express, 24 June 1995

LTTE plotted suicide bombing of Rao: report

Press Trust of India, Washington, 1 May

The Liberation Tigers of Tamil Eelam (LTTE) plotted a suicide bomb attack on Prime Minister P V Narasimha Rao in 1995, according to the US State Department's latest report on global terrorism.

It says the LTTE "conducted or planned suicide bombings against Narasimha Rao, Sri Lankan army headquarters, senior Lankan military and government officials, and government offices in Colombo."

The Tigers plagued the Sri Lankan government last year with insurgency and terrorism directed against senior political leaders, economic infrastructure-related facilities and civilians, according to the report 'Patterns of Global Terrorism in 1995'.

Indian Express, 24 June 1995

Chapter Four

Conclusions

The Sri Lanka crisis is the consequence of a festering wound from the past, which fortunately is neither malignant nor terminally cancerous. The wound that has festered had been originally inflicted by the tactics of the British imperialists when to administer the colony that Sri Lanka had become, they relied on the Tamils of the island for the purpose, and also brought to the plantations indentured Tamil labourers from India to exploit the fields. The British had by then already ruled the Madras area through the instrument of the East India Company, and hence were familiar with the Tamils and vice versa. This comprador relationship of the Tamils with the British colonialists also enabled the Tamils to make progress educationally and economically while the landed gentry and overwhelmingly rural Sinhala population languished from the expropriation and exploitation of their lands.

When Independence came to the island in 1948, the relatively more impoverished and less western educated Sinhalas took advantage of their massive majority (74 per cent of the population) to deny equal opportunity in the economy or a proportionate share in the power structure, or even recognize merit in university admissions. They tried to muscle out the Tamil language and require that all demonstrate proficiency in the Sinhala language. This is the origin of the problem of Sri Lanka today.

The Tamil community, especially the leadership of Chelvanayakam, as head of the Tamil Federal Party, tried for a negotiated settlement of the growing Tamil grievances in independent Sri Lanka as also to pacify the chauvinistic rage of the Sinhalas. But no sooner had he reached an agreement with the representative of the Sinhalas then the deal was broken, disregarded and just caricatured. As the Sinhalas got more and more aggressive in dealing the Tamils, and despairing that India seemed unconcerned about the plight of Tamils, the violent elements amongst the Tamils began gaining the upper hand and legitimacy. The turning point came in July 1983 when the Sinhala mobs, police and army went on a rampage and a killing spree. India then decided to intervene, and train the existing Tamil militant organization like the LTTE, TELO, EPRLF, PLOTE, EROS, etc..

Thus, instead of brokering peace between the Tamils and the Sinhalas, the Indian Government under the leadership of Indira Gandhi decided to train these Tamil militants in various camps in India. Most of the outfits thus trained accepted the tutelage of India and agreed to conform to inter-organizational norms of cooperation.

But the LTTE was a renegade from the very first day. Because the leading militant organization, the TELO, led by the charismatic Sri Sabarathnam, had the patronage of Indian intelligence agencies, and also initially the support of the DMK in Tamil Nadu, the irrationally jealous Prabhakaran, leading the LTTE, exploited the rivalry between Karunanidhi and M.G. Ramachandran of the AIADMK and drew logistic and monetary support from the latter.

Using that support, Prabhakaran snared Sabarathnam in the Jaffna jungles and got him assassinated. He later assassinated the leaders of other militant Tamil outfits. Soon in the vacuum, the LTTE emerged as the main and dominant militant organization. Thereafter, in the classic pattern of guerilla organizations, the LTTE began to spread using the weapons of narco-terror and by buying influence. The LTTE ferried Saddam Hussein's illegal shipments of crude oil in their tankers using Panamanian and other dubious flags, drug-running for Afghans and Thais, weapons trade for the Sicilian mafia from Palermo, and even antique smuggling for the highly placed in India. Through these ill-gotten funds, it become a purchaser of weapons in the grey and clandestine markets. Tamil diaspora whose families were in Jaffna were subject to extortion, while some others romanticized their proximity to the "leader" and paid handsomely for it. Indian politicians, academicians, journalists, lawyers, and retired diplomats began receiving donations for speaking up for the LTTE and for denouncing the opponents of the LTTE.

When the Indian Government dispatched 100,000 troops to the northern areas of Sri Lanka to safeguard the Tamils and get implemented on the ground the 1987 Indo-Sri Lanka Accord signed by Rajiv Gandhi as Prime Minister and Jayawardene as President of Sri Lanka, the LTTE disinformation machine by now well established went on an over-drive with salacious stories of the atrocities committed by the Indian Army. Their Indian stooges held rallies and published booklets within India to discredit the IPKF. Rajiv Gandhi (by now beleaguered by the Bofors scandal and the betrayal of the new President of Sri Lanka, Premadasa) agreed to withdraw the IPKF in a phased manner. However, Rajiv Gandhi lost his party's majority in the elections to Parliament in 1989, and his successor V.P. Singh, whose allies openly supported the LTTE, immediately withdrew the IPKF. The LTTE was portrayed in the anti-India media as having "defeated" the world's third largest army, and thus acquired a larger than life image. It used its hero status with a compliant Karunanidhi as Chief Minister of Tamil Nadu, to build a network of supply chains within the Tamil Nadu State. It had access to hospitals for its injured cadre, supply of diesel, kerosene, and medicines for the Jaffna supporters, small arms manufacture units in Coimbatore, a uniform stitching factory in Erode, and a modern wireless communication centre in Trichy. The second-rank leaders of the LTTE travelled freely within the state in cars using the ruling DMK party flags to evade the police.

But the situation changed soon enough. The V.P. Singh Government was toppled in 1990, and a government headed by Chandrashekhar took office. This author was the senior-most Minister in that government and perceived as the architect of the new formation. Rajiv Gandhi extended his party's support to the government. Within two months in office, the DMK Government in the state was dismissed on the ground that there was collusion of the Chief Minister with the LTTE. The LTTE supply chain was thereafter destroyed.

The problem worsened for the LTTE with the declaration of mid-term elections to Parliament. The media hype, whether genuinely misinformed, or contrived, made out that Rajiv Gandhi would return with a majority in the elections, and be Prime Minister once more. The LTTE having learnt of Rajiv Gandhi's unguarded remarks that he would "fix" the LTTE once he returned to office, Prabhakaran's plan to assassinate Rajiv Gandhi was set in motion. This is what the Supreme Court concluded.

But Prabhakaran needed to obtain two things to carry out his assassination plan successfully. First was to ensure that Rajiv Gandhi came to Tamil Nadu to be accessible to the LTTE assassins; and, second, he needed as allies some people highly placed in India, and so powerful that the blame for the assassination would not be pinned on the LTTE.

These two preconditions were understandable since trusted Tamil-speaking LTTE cadres could not move around secretly and freely anywhere in India except in Tamil Nadu and Pondicherry. Hence, the assassination had to take place in Tamil Nadu. But more importantly, seeing the popularity amongst Tamils of the Chandrashekar Government's decision to dismiss Karunanidhi's state government, the LTTE could ill-afford the stigma of Rajiv Gandhi's assassination. They had to have a powerful clique in India that could divert the investigative agencies from pursuing the LTTE as the suspects in the assassination.

The LTTE did succeed in getting Rajiv Gandhi to come to a convenient spot in Tamil Nadu, to be able to assassinate him. How that could be arranged is known. As the Jain Commission itself documents, a close circle of party office-bearers (who incidentally are Ministers today in the UPA Government) had insisted that Rajiv Gandhi return to campaign in Tamil Nadu even though during his earlier visit in April 1991 it was decided that he would not come again for the campaign. His tour programme, after it was decided and drawn up, was also not keep secret. What has not been investigated so far is whether there is a nexus between the LTTE wanting him in Tamil Nadu and the close circle insisting on his going there. This is a matter that normally should have been investigated, but the terms of reference of D.R. Kartikeyan of the Special Investigation Team (SIT) was just to determine who or which agency killed Rajiv Gandhi. On that question he did a brilliant job, and merits the highest national award for it. But investigation of the conspiracy angle was outside the scope of his inquiry.

Before I demitted office as Union Law Minister, there was set up a Commission under Justice J.S. Verma, a sitting senior judge of the Supreme Court, to go into the security lapses. It came to the conclusion that the security arrangements were adequate, but that the Congress Party local leaders disrupted and broke these arrangements. The Commission urged further in-depth inquiry into it. The successor Narasimha Rao Government declined to accept the recommendation, and the Report was shelved. Instead, those close to Ms Sonia Gandhi began to lobby for a new Commission to go into the conspiracy angle in the Rajiv Gandhi assassination. A Commission was indeed set up under Justice M.C. Jain, a retired former Chief Justice of the Delhi High Court. The Commission soon became a circus and a platform for nefarious propaganda. The proceedings were used to rubbish the reputation of Narasimha Rao and his friend, a religious preacher, and globetrotter Chandraswami. In 1991 before the assassination both Rao and Chandraswami had become very close to Rajiv Gandhi. In fact, Rajiv Gandhi used to invite Chandraswami to his living room and ask him to perform pujas. Therefore, the accusation that the duo had plotted the assassination is ludicrous. They had no motive to assassinate their benefactor. Instead those who stood to gain monetarily and politically by his assassination are the natural first suspects.

But the motive behind the inquisition by the Commission was obvious—exonerate the LTTE by throwing up bogus leads and new accusations to unsettle the SIT probe being conducted by Kartikeyan, which probe was at an advanced stage of clinching the case against the LTTE. Now, why should these "high ups" be interested in such an exoneration?

Indeed the matter gets very intriguing when all the circumstantial evidence is put together. These are:

1. Why and by whom was Rajiv Gandhi prevailed upon to go back to campaign in Tamil Nadu when the TNCC President, Vazhapadi Ramamurthy, the AIADMK leader and ally Jayalalitha, the TN Governor Bhisma Narayan Singh, and the Chandrashekhar Government were all against it?
2. How is it that not one Congress leader was in close enough proximity to Rajiv Gandhi (Verma Commission puts it as a circle within a diameter of 12 feet) to be killed or seriously injured at the detonation spot? This is curious because habitually Congress persons try to stick close to the leader of the party for a possible photo opportunity.
3. On whose authority was the NSG and CBI restrained for 14 hours from storming the hideout of the assassination mastermind, Sivarasan and others in Bangalore, which delay enabled them to commit suicide? (Thus they could not "sing" for the authorities during a future interrogation about the facts about the assassination.)

4. Why has the Congress Party showed no interest in obtaining the extradition of the proclaimed offenders Prabhakaran and Pottu Amman?
5. How is it defensible for the party to have an open political alliance with those who have acted at the behest of the LTTE such as the DMK, PMK, MDMK and the Dalit Panthers? How did the Delhi Government come to award one acre of land next to the Indira Gandhi International Airport in Delhi plus a lakh of rupees to the Dravida Kazhagam, an avowed supporter of the LTTE which does not have a single member in the Delhi area?

The Rajiv Gandhi assassination is an important question of national security for Indians. Can we tolerate a foreign terrorist organization killing a leader in our country simply because his policies were not to their liking? More important, can we be safe if those within our country can contract with a terrorist organization to kill those inconvenient for them? And most important can we allow such a terrorist organization to strike roots in our neighbourhood and have a terror infrastructure that can vitiate the democratic politics of India with money, narcotics, and plain murder?

Hence, the lessons from the assassination of Rajiv Gandhi have to be learnt well. The Indian viewpoint on the Sri Lanka crisis has to take into account these national security aspects. India's options have to be based on the minimum condition of excluding the LTTE from any role in a future set-up in Sri Lanka.

The LTTE, thus, *is part of the problem, and not a part of the solution.* In the search for a feasible and sustainable solution, India's option must include the eradication of the problem.

Part of the problem is the inability of the Sinhala majority to share power with the Tamil minority. Such a sharing can be best done in a Constitution with sufficient devolution—by replacing the present unitary Sri Lankan one with a quasi-federal

Indian type or fully federal US type. The recent decision (on 23 October 2006) of the Sri Lankan ruling party, the SLFP, to sign an "MoU" with the leading opposition party, the UNP, to seek ways for devolution in the Constitution, acceptable to all communities—Sinhala, Tamil, and those who want to be identified not as Tamils, but as Muslims—is therefore, welcome. The JVP, which has stayed out because this MoU does not de-notify the Cease-fire Agreement (CFA) and abandon "peace talks" with the LTTE, should be brought on board by conceding these two reasonable demands.

The Sri Lankan Government has made a grievous mistake by submitting to Norwegian pressure and thereby agreeing to attend the so-called peace talks with the LTTE at Geneva. The so-called peace talks can have no other outcome except to legitimize a terrorist organization which the LTTE had been declared internationally. Therefore, it is banned in a number of countries as a terrorist organization.

The so-called peace talks are engineered by the Norwegians who are for private and pecuniary reasons committed to the LTTE. It is shocking to learn that the Norwegian Chief Negotiator presented a 6-foot TV to Prabhakaran completely viating his impartial status. The Norwegians moreover have no clue about the real origin of the problem in Sri Lanka. Hence, to designate them as mediators is ridiculous on the part of the Sri Lankan Government. The Norwegians ought to be sent home.

In any case, since the LTTE is part of the problem and is not acceptable to any patriotic Indian, even remotely, as part of the solution, hence, the so-called peace talks in Geneva is against Indian interest as well as against the interest of the international struggle against terrorism. Therefore, I suggest to the short-sighted weak-kneed Sri Lankan leadership in Government to fall in line with the JVP insistence not to participate in any more peace talks. Instead, the Sri Lankan Parliament should adopt a resolution to replace the present unitary Constitution with a federal or a quasi-federal Constitution that will meet the legitimate aspirations of the Tamil people of the island.

Tamils and Sinhalas are one people. They have the same DNA structure. There is thus no ethnic difference between them. They all had originated in the Indian mainland: speak sister languages, Sinhala and Tamil, with a large vocabulary in common with Sanskrit and Pali, both Indian languages. Their scripts have both evolved from the Brahmi script. Thus, there is no fundamental linguistic difference. Their religions, Hinduism and Buddhism, believe in the same distinguishing and fundamental theology of *darshan,* re-incarnation and *karma.* In fact, Buddhism began as a reform movement of Hinduism and these reforms have been absorbed by Hinduism. Hence, there is fundamentally no religious difference between a Sinhala Buddhist and a Tamil Hindu.

The two communities grew apart during the colonial period because the Tamils had access to the British imperialist invaders, due to the latter's earlier contacts with Tamils on the Indian mainland. This gave the Tamils professional and educational advantages. Upon getting Independence the Sinhala majority used their brute majority to try and close the gap by undermocratic equalization procedures and denying power to the Tamils by adopting a unitary constitution that had no safeguards for the Tamil minority. This, of course, backfired—in fact, it has landed Sri Lanka in the present spiraling crisis.

The way out today, consistent with India's national security aims, is for Sri Lanka to immediately adopt a resolution in its Parliament to implement a devolved Constitution, and for India then to intervene to finish off the LTTE menace. The US, China and Israel, nations which can contribute for the implementation of this solution, must back India in this structured intervention.

Index

INDIA AND SRI LANKA

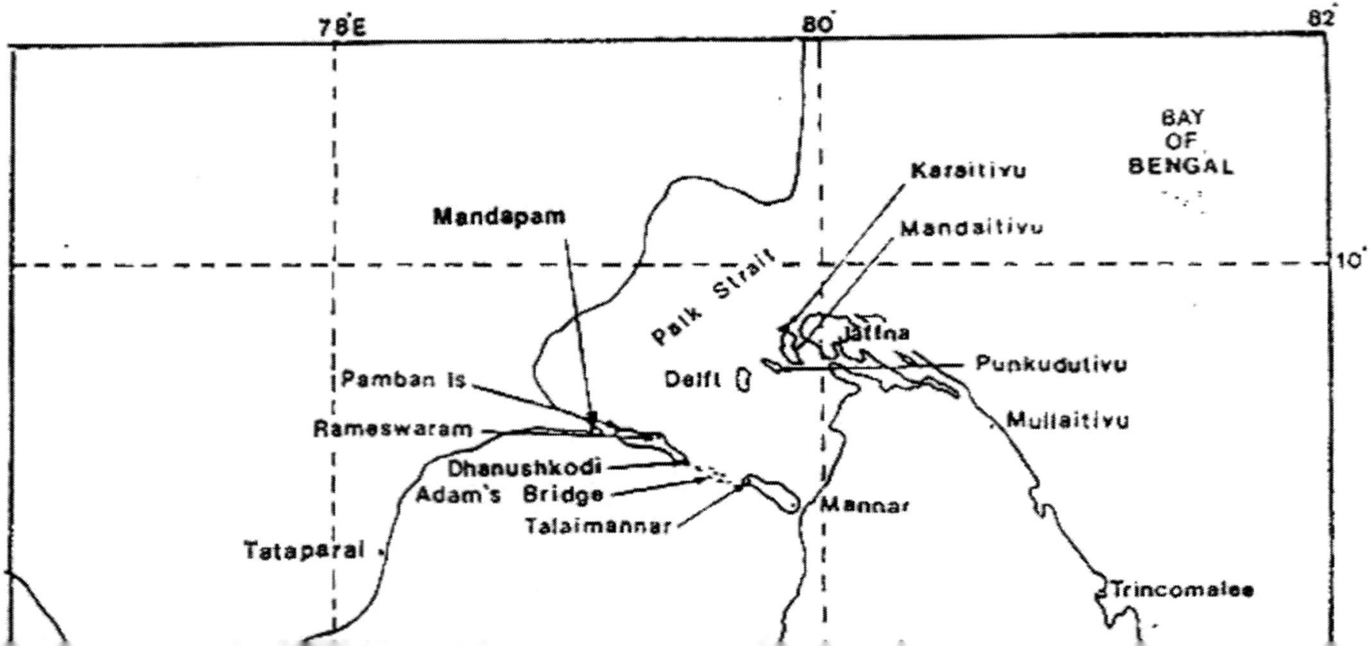

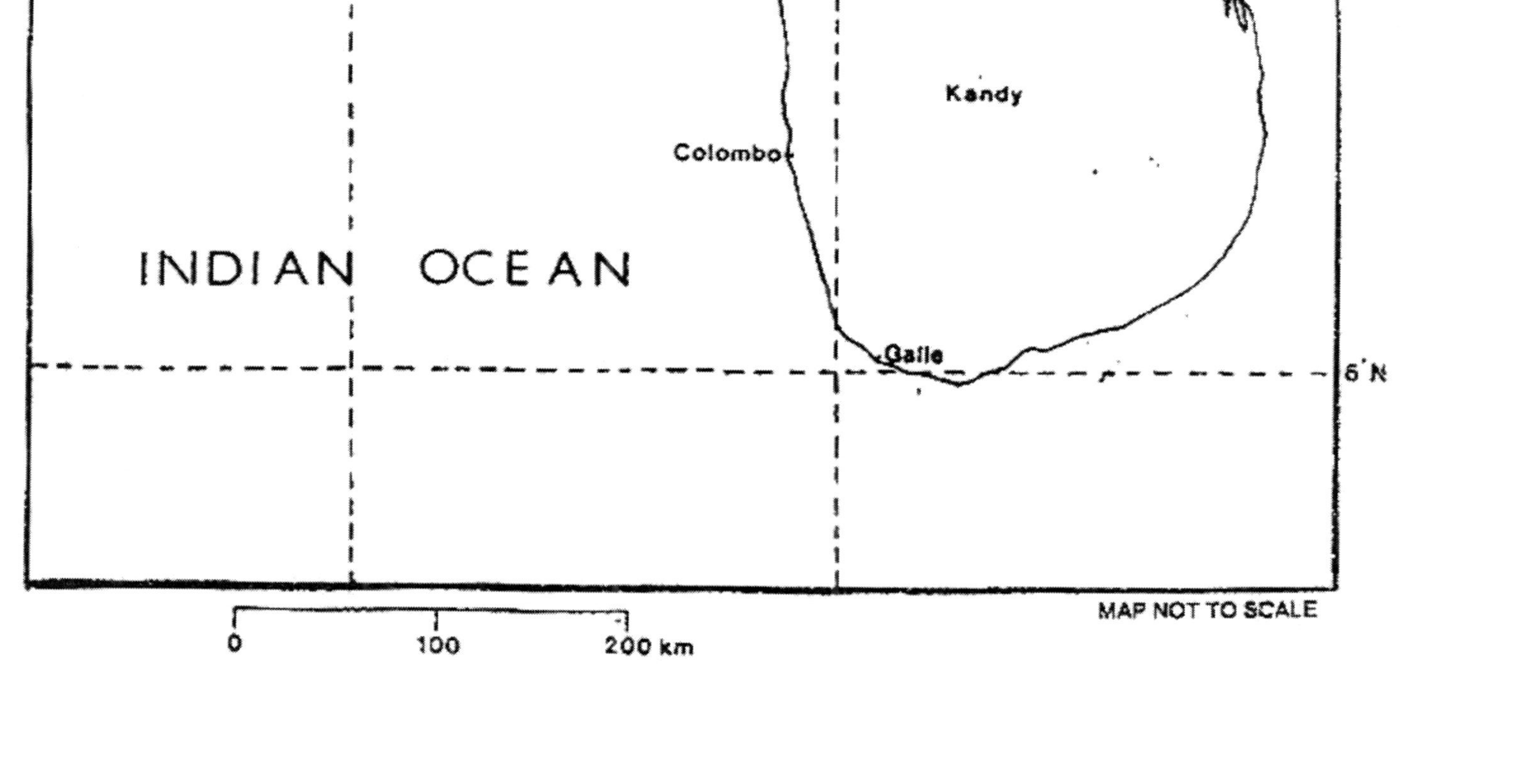
Batticaloa
Kandy
Colombo
INDIAN OCEAN
Galle
6°N
MAP NOT TO SCALE
0
100
200 km